Puffin Books

The Puffin Book

GW00871061

Track and field athletics is both the most international
of all sports and the centre-piece of the modern
Olympic Games. Running, jumping, throwing and
hurdling attract hundreds of thousands of competitors all
over the world and millions of television viewers follow
the victories and record-breaking feats of the very best.

Neil Allen's *Puffin Book of Athletics* traces the history of
this sport, beginning with the Games of the ancient
Greeks, and then shows how athletics was revitalized in
nineteenth-century Britain. The story of athletics in the
modern Olympics, including many of the fiercest
controversies of the time, is followed by pen pictures of
the greatest champions, a guide to the techniques of the
various events and a full statistical section of world
records and gold medal winners.

The author, who still jogs for fitness himself, has
reported six Olympic Games as a journalist and was
president of the International Athletics Writers until
1978.

An essential book for all those interested in the 1980
Moscow Olympic Games and beyond.

Neil Allen

The Puffin Book of
Athletics

Puffin Books

Puffin Books,
Penguin Books Ltd, Harmondsworth,
Middlesex, England
Penguin Books, 625 Madison Avenue,
New York, New York 10022, U.S.A.
Penguin Books Australia Ltd, Ringwood,
Victoria, Australia
Penguin Books Canada Ltd, 2801 John Street,
Markham, Ontario, Canada L3R 1B4
Penguin Books (N.Z.) Ltd, 182–190 Wairau Road,
Auckland 10, New Zealand

Published in Puffin Books 1980

Copyright © Neil Allen 1980
All rights reserved

Typeset, printed and bound in Great Britain by
Hazell Watson & Viney Ltd,
Aylesbury, Bucks
Set in Monotype Times Roman

Except in the United States of America, this
book is sold subject to the condition that
it shall not, by way of trade or otherwise, be lent,
re-sold, hired out, or otherwise circulated without
the publisher's prior consent in any form of
binding or cover other than that in which it is
published and without a similar condition
including this condition being imposed on the
subsequent purchaser

For Matthew and James

Contents

Foreword by Sebastian Coe

Let us talk athletics or, more specifically, what I know about best – middle-distance running. To many runners it is their whole way of life, and a good way of life it is, too. But to me, I should emphasize, it has only been *half* my life.

This is because it is worth remembering that, great though you might become through talent and dedication, it cannot and will not go on for ever. You will want to have something besides memories when the time comes to quit.

Hard work in athletics is certainly not inconsistent with fun. There are the laughs that sometimes go with the long runs and tough training sessions with good friends. There are wry smiles in defeat, too, although they tend to come later when the hurt and disappointment have passed away.

But whether your enjoyment comes from the laughs and company of club life, or from the joy of success after painful application, there must be some fun in the endeavour.

We cannot choose our forefathers so we cannot choose our share of natural ability. But what we can do is to work hard and maximize our talent so that we enjoy the deep satisfaction which comes from doing our best at anything.

There is no way to the top that is free from some disappointments. As you will discover in the historical section of Neil Allen's book, all the 'greats' have had their defeats and learnt from them.

When we are young, even in our late teens, we all have differing rates of physical development. Some youngsters, therefore, may be stronger than others at a particular age, but not necessarily for ever. If your performances in track and field sometimes seem inconsistent, please bear in mind that your years as school and junior athletes will require patience and determination.

Now a word or two of friendly advice. Do not be in too great a hurry to pick your coach, and choose carefully when you do. You should have a personal coach by the time you are eighteen; until then membership of a good club should help you not to get set in bad habits or inefficient techniques. Remember a coach must be someone you can admire and respect. Accepting a coach means accepting authority. He or she must have your full respect and obedience, so it is better to be late in choosing your coach than to make the wrong choice.

Athletics coaching today, if it is to be successful, must be science-based. But science cannot supply all the answers, and so coaching is also an art. So is sport at its highest level. Neil Allen reminds me that after I beat the world mile record I said: 'I run unconsciously, as if I am on automatic pilot. I am afraid it is something you have or you don't.'

Now injuries. For sprinters and field events specialists, injuries may come in many ways, including incorrect technique or failing to warm up before training and competition. For middle- and long-distance runners, the most common cause is over-use: too much, too soon of anything is bad for anyone, be it money, success or, in the case of a runner, mileage. Quality before quantity is a generalization but I believe it to be true.

So select your goals carefully. Choose your races and competitions wisely, be patient, and above all think about what you are doing. Just like the great champions of the past and present whose feats Neil Allen records in this book.

The athlete should always have an open mind. What are you doing? Why? Is it effective? Your coach should be able to satisfy you on these counts. But certainly don't train if you don't feel right and never hurry an injury. Time is on your side if you will let it be. Better to lose even a whole year, as I did with stress fractures, than lose a career through permanent damage.

Finally, whether you are an enthusiastic spectator or an ambitious young athlete, good luck and sincerest good wishes in your sport.

Sebastian Coe

1 How Athletics Began

Track and field athletics is certainly older than recorded history. For as long as there have been young men and women on this earth, they have enjoyed running, jumping and throwing, either by themselves or against each other to find out who is the best.

From these informal contests amongst families and friends, many thousands of years ago, has come the present vast amount of organized competition on every continent, with hundreds of thousands of athletes starting at school or club level in the hope of one day representing their country in major meetings such as the European Championships and the Commonwealth or Olympic Games.

The International Amateur Athletic Federation, the governing body of the sport, was founded at a meeting in Stockholm in 1912 attended by seventeen countries, and now has a total of 162 countries – the largest membership of any international federation in sport.

Athletics is the centre-piece of the summer Olympic Games. In addition, the IAAF hold their own World Cup and World Championships as well as official Indoor and Cross-Country Championships.

From about 3,500 years BC we have evidence, from sculpture, of the Egyptians practising running and jumping. But it was the ancient Greeks, whose sophisticated society placed considerable emphasis on physical prowess as well as learning, who had most influence upon the shape of modern athletics.

We cannot be sure of the exact rules of their Pythian, Nemean, Isthmian, and, eventually, Olympic Games. But the chief events included the *stade* (sprint), from which comes the word stadium, *diaulos* (long sprint), *dolichos* (long-distance run) and the all-round test of the *pentathlon* – consisting of long jump, javelin, discus, sprint and wrestling events.

The Greeks who competed at Olympia, a stadium on a plain in the southern province of Elis, had a starting gate controlled by ropes held by the official starter. If any sprinter made what we now call a 'false' start, the punishment was a whipping.

The first Olympic champion we know by name was Coroebus. In the Olympia Games of 776 BC he won the straight *stade* or sprint race over a distance of about 180 metres, close enough to our 200 metres run round one curve of the modern 400 metres track.

We have some more evidence of these ancient athletics. The pentathlon was decided on the number of first places gained in five events. Long jumpers often carried small weights in their hands to heave themselves forward and it has been suggested that they made not one leap but a multiple jump, rather like the present-day triple jump. The Greek javelin thrower was allowed to put his fingers through the loop of a leather thong at the end of his light wooden spear so that he could achieve greater pulling power.

As we shall see later, the Games of ancient Greece greatly stimulated the modern revival of the Olympics, although they had fallen into decline and were eventually abolished by the decree of the Roman Emperor Theodosius. But, however rich the inheritance from the distant past, it is true to say, in the words of the athletics historian Dr Roberto Quercetani, that 'Track and field athletics, as we know it today, was born in the British Isles'.

Dr Quercetani was not thinking primarily of the

Tailteann Games of Ireland, which survived until about AD 1168 or of Scotland's various Highland Games which can be traced back to the early fourteenth century; he was considering the great interest in professional 'pedestrianism' in England in the eighteenth and nineteenth centuries, and the subsequent growth of amateur athletics in the schools and universities.

The first outstanding athletes of Britain were to be found, nearly two hundred years ago, in the ranks of footmen, pottery workers, farm labourers, barmen and bricklayers. These jobs brought in little money and strong young men were therefore eager to win a lump sum of cash from a sporting wager, generally made by gentlemen of independent financial means.

There was no controlling body in athletics then and the only firm rule was that bets should always be paid promptly. Pierce Egan, the leading sports writer of the nineteenth century, some of whose semi-fictitious characters were borrowed by Charles Dickens, reported thus a 150 yards sprint race between Leach and Shaw in February 1818 on a road near London's Epping Forest:

More betting took place on the spot than has been witnessed for the last twenty years. The ground was roped with stakes, to prevent the crowd from pressing upon them and also a rope with stakes was placed down the middle to prevent their jostling with each other.

At two o'clock the signal was given and Leach got the start by nearly a yard. But Shaw soon shot by him like an arrow and when he touched the handkerchief Leach was at least seven and a half yards behind him. The 150 yards were accomplished in the very short space of 16 seconds.

Leach ran without shoes and had only a short pair of drawers. The countryman Shaw was as lightly clad, excepting a pair of half-boots. Shaw bids fair to beat all England – he gets over the ground with the fleetness of a greyhound. For 400 guineas.

The feverish betting could lead to some rough interference with the racing, as we see from this comment by Egan after Blumsell, a painter by trade, had run nine and a quarter miles in less than an hour: 'Unfair means were used to prevent his winning: particularly the interruption of a man who twice crossed him and whom Blumsell collared and ultimately floored.' Today's television commentators would surely be in danger of fracturing their vocal cords at such a sight.

From all these near-anonymous professional 'peds' we can cite two great champions. One was Foster Powell, an attorney's clerk from Yorkshire, who was born in 1736. Another was Captain Robert Barclay Allardice, a Scottish landowner, born in 1779. Both were famed as long-distance walkers, although they ran as well, and Barclay trained and boxed with some of the champion bare-fist pugilists.

Their life styles were obviously very different, but in both cases they prepared them naturally for their athletic feats. Powell became accustomed to walking long distances when going on journeys to obtain leases for his employers, while Captain Barclay would ride and walk many miles both when hunting and surveying his considerable estates.

Powell, who was renowned for his honesty in a sport then often marred by double-crosses, walked 100 miles in 22 hours in 1789, and more than 400 miles in just over five and a half days when he was fifty-six years old. Barclay, of whom it was claimed, 'his knowledge of the capabilities of the human frame is complete', covered 1,000 miles in 1,000 consecutive hours in 1808 and so earned himself the vast sum, in those days, of 1,000 guineas.

These efforts created so much public interest that Powell is reported to have visited Switzerland and France for exhibitions and Barclay's record-breaking led to the publication of an athletics training book by Walter Thom in 1813. The author's recommended diet for the young sportsman was beef, stale bread, mutton, strong beer and salts – fish, vegetables, cheese, butter and eggs being forbidden. Sweating under loads of bed-clothes and the taking of laxative medicines were both advised.

When Barclay was competing there was no real distinction between professionals and amateurs, although regular and genuine amateur meetings were held by those attending the Royal Military Academy, Sandhurst, from about 1812. Professional athletes continued to be household names, including Billy Jackson, who in 1845 became the first man to run 11 miles within an hour, and an American Indian, nicknamed Deerfoot, who arrived in Britain in 1861. Deerfoot, whose given name was Louis Bennet, was then already thirty-five and rather solidly built for a distance runner. But thousands paid to see him run in moccasins and breech cloth, with a single feather in his hair, and to applaud his undoubted courage and extraordinary natural ability.

With comparatively little training, Deerfoot ran 10 miles in 51 min. 26 sec., a time not beaten for twenty-one years, and covered 11 miles 970 yds in an hour – this was not to be surpassed by anyone for another thirty-four years. With his livelihood at stake, and promoters wanting their money's worth, Deerfoot raced and travelled far too much to do himself justice. But when he left Britain in 1863 he took with him a silver belt inscribed to his 'unequalled powers as a runner and his modest and gentle manner, which won admiration through the kingdom'.

Although there was at least one important postscript, Deerfoot's tour was really the last flourish of professional athletics in Britain. Changes were taking place, through a new, vital influence which can be traced back to a social evening at Exeter College, Oxford University in 1850.

In the rooms of a young man, Halifax Wyatt, a group of undergraduates were complaining about the inadequacies of the horses they had ridden during the day's college steeplechase. Spontaneously, they decided to have a two-mile race across country on *foot*. From this light-hearted proposal came an 'Exeter Autumn Meeting' of flat and hurdles races. The competitors in the mile were handicapped like race-horses with several pounds of shot carried in a belt round their waists.

In 1864 the first athletics match was held between the amateurs of Oxford and Cambridge Universities. Winning individual performances included 10·5 sec. in the 100 yards, 4 min. 56 sec. in the mile (the same time as that credited to the professional, Captain Barclay), 17¾ sec. in the 120 yards hurdles, 1·65 m in the high jump and 5·49 m in the long jump.

In the same year, 1864, the Mincing Lane Athletic Club was formed. Later it became the London AC. Slowly, and sometimes painfully, because the code of strict amateurism has never been easy to follow, athletes from the universities and from the working classes were to be united under a single amateur governing body.

In 1880 the Amateur Athletic Association was formed at Oxford and the way was open for anyone to compete provided they could be described as 'a person who has never competed for money with or against a professional for any prize and who has never taught, pursued or assisted in the practice of athletic exercises as a means of obtaining a livelihood'. The Amateur Athletic Union of America was formed in the same year.

The last surge in the now dwindling professional side of the sport in Britain came in 1886, when Walter Goodall George, the foremost middle-distance and distance runner of the time, was forced to turn professional because he was more than £1,000 in debt. George, born in Wiltshire in 1858, had run the fastest mile ever recorded by an amateur – 4 min. 23·2 sec. As a professional, his obvious rival was Bill Cummings of Scotland, whose best time was 4 min. 16·2 sec.

Their rivalry was put to the test on 23 August 1886, at Lillie Bridge, when George won in 4 min. 12¾ sec., with Cummings collapsing sixty yards before the finish.

No amateur or professional was to run a mile faster than that for another twenty-nine years. But George himself had done even better – in 1885, in a paced time trial in London witnessed by a leading reporter, he had covered the mile in 4 min. 10·2 sec.

Once George's heyday was over, amateur athletics, internationally as well as in Britain, continued to grow unchecked. In 1895 the New York AC gave a thorough beating to the London AC at a meeting in New York, when the 12,000 spectators saw three world records beaten and one equalled.

It should be added that one of the major benefits of organized amateur athletics was that, unlike professional promotions, it gave space, even in its earlier programmes, to the field events and hurdles, as well as the more popular sprints and distance races.

Just as well, too, for standards in the field were still far from being as firmly developed as those in running. By the end of 1895, on the eve of the launching of the modern Olympics, the world's best performances included a high jump of 1·97 m, a pole vault of only 3·48 m and a long jump of 7·21 m. The best achievement in the throwing events were 14·32 m for the shot, 44·46 m for the hammer and 44 m with the javelin. Field events were handicapped by lack of popularity, disagreement about the rules and a need for improvement both in facilities and in technique.

The basic framework for high hurdling – to take just one example to illustrate the conditions in the early days – was laid down quite arbitrarily. The Committee which administered the first Oxford–Cambridge match decided on a 120 yd race with ten flights of 3 ft 6 in. (1·07 m) sheep hurdles staked firmly into the ground. The athlete knew that he could not risk hitting such solid obstacles and was therefore forced to jump high, landing with both feet together, so that there was an almost dead stop after each hurdle. Nowadays the hurdles are lightweight barriers and the hurdler sprints smoothly over them, knowing that they will topple forward easily if clipped.

By the end of the last century, however, both track and field athletics were becoming far more streamlined compared with the earlier rugged pioneering days. Amateur governing bodies were set up, not only in Britain and the United States, but also in Sweden, Germany, France, New Zealand, Belgium and Canada. The mood was now ready for a widening of the international stage. The opportunity came in 1896 when the first of the modern Olympic Games was held in Athens.

2 Athletics and the Olympic Games

Pierre de Fredi, Baron de Coubertin, a French aristocrat and writer on education, was convinced that his countrymen needed to be shaken out of their apathy. (They had been defeated in the Franco–Prussian War of 1870–71.) His government invited him to study physical education throughout the world and in 1887, when he was twenty-four, he visited England. Inspired by Thomas Hughes's novel, *Tom Brown's Schooldays*, he decided that what was needed was a combination of sturdy British manliness and some of the ideals of the ancient Greek Olympics, and he became enthusiastic about the idea of reviving the Olympic Games. After a long struggle his determination was rewarded by the staging, in 1896, of the first modern Games in the Greek capital, Athens.

Athens, 1896

The athletics events were held in the venerable stadium of Herodis, which dated back to about 300 BC and had been in ruins until it was excavated in 1870. The huge cost of rebuilding the stadium was paid partly by public subscription, partly by a subsidy from George Averoff, a Greek citizen from Alexandria.

As well as money, expertise was required. At comparatively short notice the Greeks turned to Charles Perry, the groundsman at London's Stamford Bridge, then famous for athletics and now the home of Chelsea Football Club.

Because it had to fit into the restricted area of the ancient stadium, the track measured 333·3 m; the turns were so sharp that it was impossible to achieve good times in the 400 metres. (The organizers wisely decided to do without a 200 metres race because of the danger of falling.) Perry was also handicapped by the lack of proper materials and a shortage of water, and had to build the track with a loose surface.

There was no background, as there is now, of months, even years, of preparation devoted to the Olympics. The Athens Games was opened on 6 April 1896 by Prince George of Greece and caught the international athletes of the day by surprise. Nobody had told the Americans, for example, that the Greeks had not put their calendar forward by eleven days, as had most western countries, in 1752. When the United States team of ten athletes left by boat for Athens they believed that they had allowed at least two weeks on arrival for training. Even so, they won nine out of the ten events for which they had entered.

The American victories included the discus, which had been regarded as a Greek speciality. The unexpected champion was Robert Garratt from Princeton University, who had been practising with a crude home-made discus in the States and then found when he got to Athens that it was heavier than the type used for the Olympic competition. His strength, rather than style, brought him success in this event and the shot, and he also came second in the long jump.

Edwin (Teddy) Flack was another notable champion, with victories in both the 800 metres and 1,500 metres. He was an Australian studying accountancy in London, who, having heard rumours that the Olympics were to be revived, took a month's holiday and arrived in Athens to share a room (there was no Olympic Village for competitors until

1932) with George Stuart-Robertson, an Oxford graduate and discus thrower who was to win an Olympic prize for a Greek ode.

They lived casually as tourists, without any of the pressure which can now weigh so heavily upon Olympic athletes 'hunting for gold'. Once, Flack wrote to his friends, he and George threw the dishwater out of their window only to find it had soaked a smartly dressed Greek passer-by. Incidentally, because Flack was a member of the London A C working in Britain, it was Britain, not Australia, which initially gained the credit for his victories.

Although he had never raced further than ten miles in his life, Teddy Flack decided to take part in the marathon which was to be run from the bridge of the village of Marathon to the stadium in Athens, a distance of 40,000 m. Flack wanted to run because, as he wrote home, there was such an 'interest' in the event.

That was not surprising. Marathon is famous as the scene of the Greek victory over the Persian army in 490 BC, and the story of the Greek hero Pheidippides who ran all the way from Marathon to Athens with the news and then died with the word 'Victory' on his lips.

Imagine then the cheers that rang out when the Greeks, who had not won any other Olympic athletics event, filled the 70,000-capacity stadium to cheer home Spiridon Louis, a village postman, as the marathon champion. He had carefully held back from the pace which was set first by Lermusiaux of France and then by Flack, both of whom failed to finish, and pulled away over the last 5,000 metres. Never has there been a more joyful welcome for an Olympic winner. He was followed into the stadium by a mounted band; women tore off their jewellery to throw at his feet; the Crown Princes of Greece jogged alongside him to the finish. Amongst his subsequent rewards from a grateful nation, Louis received a voucher for 365 meals, free shoe-polishing for life, and a plot of ground thereafter known as the 'Field of Marathon'.

Another Greek, Velokas, finished third, but the Hungarian, Gyula Kellner, who was running behind him, said that he had seen Velokas get out of a carriage. When Velokas sadly admitted he had taken a lift his national singlet was ripped from his back and he was disqualified. Kellner was officially awarded third place and was given a gold watch in compensation as well.

Paris, 1900

This time the Olympics coincided with the World Fair and the building of the Eiffel Tower. The organization was so inefficient that de Coubertin himself resigned from the committee. Even the title of Olympic Games was at first abandoned, as if the French were indifferent to the high ideals of their athletes.

The so-called 'athletics track' was a 500 m circuit at the Racing Club de France in the Bois de Boulogne. It was bumpy, with an unmistakeable dip along the 100 m stretch; the take-off for the jumping was loose; the competitions dragged on for nearly five months, and some American athletes refused, on religious grounds, to compete on a Sunday. Events for professionals, termed 'world non-amateur championships', were also staged.

In spite of all the confusion and controversy there were some outstanding athletes, headed by the Americans Alvin Kraenzlein and Ray Ewry. Kraenzlein won the 60 metres sprint, the 110 and 200 metres hurdles, and the long jump. He was regarded as a pioneer in modern hurdling technique, with excellent basic speed, a straight leading leg and a forward lunge of the body. Ray Ewry won the standing high and long jumps, no longer practised in major athletics, and the triple jump. He was then thirty-five; even more remarkable was the fact that as a boy he had been seriously ill and had been advised by a doctor to take up sport to strengthen his legs.

Britain sent only five athletes to Paris. Charles Bennett, a national cross-country champion from Finchley Harriers, won the 1,500 metres in 4 min. 6·2 sec., the fastest time yet recorded, and led Britain to victory in the 5,000 metres team race. Another member of that 5,000 metres team was Frank Tysoe who also won the 800 metres with a fast second lap.

St Louis, 1904

Mainly because of the travel costs there was a slim international entry, with Britain sending no competitors at all and only Germany, Greece, Hungary and Ireland, apart from the all-conquering American hosts, being truly represented. The United States won twenty-two out of twenty-four events and sixty-eight out of seventy-two medals.

The Games were held in conjunction with the St Louis World Exhibition and were followed by so-called 'anthropological events', in which untrained negroes and American Indians were sent out to earn the laughter of the crowd as, for example, a pygmy strove mightily to achieve a shot put of about 3 m.

This humiliating circus was a grubby postscript to the high standard of the real Olympic athletics. Four Americans, Archie Hahn (60, 100 and 200 metres sprints), James Lightbody (2,500 metres steeplechase, 800 and 1,500 metres), Ray Ewry, the human rubber ball (three standing jumps), and

Harry Hillman (200 and 400 metres hurdles and 400 metres flat) won three gold medals each. The huge American Ralph Rose set a new world's record in the shot put with 14·81 m.

The biggest controversy concerned the marathon. After about 15,000 m of the 40,000 metres course one of the leaders, Fred Lorz from New York, had to give up through cramp. He obtained a lift in a passing car going towards the stadium but, claiming that he was feeling better, got out and ran on. Entering the stadium first, he was given a rapturous reception by the crowd and posed for photographs with the daughter of the American President, but he was disqualified when Thomas Hicks, the first to complete the distance on foot, came in six minutes ahead of the next genuine runner.

London, 1908

An important turning-point in the progress of the Olympics came in London in 1908 although the Games were also to be the occasion of some bitter disputes between the Americans and their British hosts. The scene was the White City in West London – a banked concrete cycle course encircling a 536·45 m track, which in turn enclosed an open-air, 100 m long swimming pool. Altogether a far more fitting setting for modern sport than the three previous ones.

The most impressive champion was the American Melvin Sheppard who won both the 800 metres, after a fast first lap, in the world record time of 1 min. 52·8 sec. and the 1,500 metres, as well as helping the United States win the medley relay.

The most disputed victory of all was that of Wyndham Halswelle of Britain in the 400 metres. In the 'first' final the American John Carpenter had been first across the finish line, but only after he had apparently impeded Halswelle (no lanes were used in those days). The officials had broken the tape and attempted to wave the runners to a halt. Carpenter was disqualified and a re-run, ordered for two days later, was boycotted by the Americans, leaving Halswelle to 'run over' in 50 sec., compared with the Olympic record of 48·4 sec. he had set in the semi-finals.

The end of the 1908 marathon was to provide one of the most memorable of all Olympic stories. It had originally been planned that the race would be run over 26 miles exactly, from Windsor Castle to White City, but then it was changed to 26 miles 385 yds (42,195 m) so that the finish would be opposite the Royal Box. That odd distance remains standard for the marathon to this day.

First into the stadium was Dorando Pietri of Italy, an experienced runner who had spurted ahead at a late stage. On entering the arena he was so dazed and confused that he turned to his right, instead of his left and then collapsed. Officials and doctors came to his aid and helped him up. After falling several more times, he was assisted across the finish line.

Not surprisingly, an official protest by the Americans led to the second man home, John Hayes of the United States, being declared the winner and the unfortunate Pietri was taken to hospital to recover. His plight created so much public sympathy, however, that he was subsequently presented with a handsome trophy by Queen Alexandra.

Only a few days later, at a banquet in London, Baron de Coubertin remarked: 'Last Sunday, during the sermon at St Paul's in honour of the athletes, the Bishop of Pennsylvania made the point "the important thing in these Olympics is not so much winning as taking part". The important thing in life is not the victory but the battle. The essential thing is not to have conquered but to have been a good loser.'

Stockholm, 1912

De Coubertin, in spite of the success of the London Games, declared that 'the Olympics must not be so comprehensive, the Games must be kept more purely athletic'. He got his wish in Stockholm where the Swedes created a splendid red-brick stadium which, to this day, gives the impression of being a medieval castle waiting for jousting knights.

The magnificent track of 383 metres was again constructed by the English groundsman Charles Perry. The field events had better facilities than ever before, including a safety-net for the hammer and cinder circles for shot and discus; the 400 metres was run in lanes; timings were accurate to a tenth of a second. Indeed, the Swedes proved that they understood track and field better than any of the previous Olympic hosts.

The hero of the Stockholm athletics was Jim Thorpe, an American Indian who won both the pentathlon and decathlon as well as finishing fourth in the individual high jump. His Indian name was Wa-tho-huck, meaning 'Bright Path'. He had been a fine player of American football and baseball at Carlile Indian College, but these American sports meant nothing to the Europeans and they did not appreciate, until he competed in the Olympic stadium, what a remarkably talented athlete he was. To take just one example, after the Olympics had finished, Thorpe defeated the high hurdles gold-medal winner, Fred Kelly, and equalled the then world record.

Sadly, Jim Thorpe is remembered best in Olympic history for his eventual disqualification, long after the Games were over, on the grounds that in 1909 he had been paid for playing professional baseball during the college vacation. Thorpe had to return his Olympic gold medals, but the runners-up sportingly refused to accept them.

In Stockholm the American athletes won victories in all

the track events up to and including the 800 metres. But in the 1,500 metres Britain's Arnold Strode Jackson produced a powerful finish to win by just one tenth of a second.

The great distance runner proved to be Hannes Kolehmainen of Finland, who won both the 5,000 and 10,000 metres and the 8,000 metres cross-country. Kolehmainen's hardest task came in the 5,000 metres where he was only a metre ahead of Jean Bouin of France as both smashed the previous world record. His pleasure in his victory was a little diluted, however, because the Finns, not then fully independent, had to wear the colours of their political overlords, Tsarist Russia, during the Games.

Antwerp, 1920

The 1916 Olympics, planned for Berlin, had to be cancelled because of the First World War.

Belgium had a hard task in trying to stage the Games in 1920. The track for the athletics, for the first time in the Olympics, was a 400 metres circuit but it was not fast and became even slower because it rained a great deal.

The morale of the American team was lowered by arguments over travel arrangements and living accommodation, as well as by the weather, and the athletics victories were this time spread much more widely among the other countries. Bevil Rudd of South Africa took the 400 metres and Albert Hill of Britain, thirty-one years old and with three years' war service with the Army in France, achieved the magnificent double of victories in the 800 and 1,500 metres within three days.

Finland's greatest moment came at the end of the marathon when Hannes Kolehmainen, double track victor in 1912, crossed the finish first in 2 hr 32 min. 35·8 sec.

Kolehmainen, his country's independence now secure, ran a victory lap wrapped in a huge Finnish flag. Paavo Nurmi, the most famous of all the 'Flying Finns', took the 10,000 metres.

Paris, 1924

The athletics events were staged at the newly enlarged Colombes Stadium, on a 500 m track. The Americans were tipped to win the sprints, but Britain's Harold Abrahams, from Cambridge University, surprised the spectators by taking the 100 metres in splendid style and Eric Liddell, a divinity student at Edinburgh who was also a rugby international, ran away with the 400 metres. Douglas Lowe, only twenty-one and like Abrahams a Cambridge undergraduate, won the 800 metres.

Nevertheless, the Americans had much more to be pleased about than they had at Antwerp. They won the 200 metres, both hurdles events and both relays, and took fifteen out of a maximum twenty-four medals in the eight field events, as well as an unexpected world-record long jump of 7·765 m in the pentathlon by Robert Le Gendre.

The supreme champion of the Games was undoubtedly Paavo Nurmi. On one afternoon, with an interval of only seventy-five minutes, the poker-faced Finn won first the 1,500 and then the 5,000 metres. Nurmi, now twenty-seven, was also first home in the 3,000 metres team race and the 10,000 metres cross-country on a day when the temperature was 45° C.

Nurmi was a great believer in economy of pace and often carried a stop-watch while he was racing. The French spectators regarded him as superhuman and, considering the way he out-ran the opposition, who could blame them?

Amsterdam, 1928

Forty-eight countries and more than 3,000 competitors were entered for the 1928 Games. Women athletes were allowed to compete for the first time, after a vote of fifteen to six by the International Olympic Committee. Their limited programme consisted of 100 metres, 4×100 metres relay, high jump, discus and 800 metres. Unfortunately, some of the women were not sufficiently prepared for the 800 metres – which was won by Lina Radke of Germany in 2 min. 16·8 sec. – and their distressed condition at the finish, caused this event to be removed from the Olympic programme until 1960.

A 400 m track was regarded as standard from 1928 on. The supreme sprinter at Amsterdam was a nineteen-year-old Canadian, Percy Williams, who won both the 100 and 200 metres. After tests by Dutch doctors of more than 3,000 Olympic competitors, Williams was announced as *the* perfect physical specimen. Douglas Lowe, showing perfect judgement, retained the 800 metres title for Britain and another product of Cambridge University, Lord Burghley, won the 400 metres hurdles after taking the lead early in the race.

The Americans gained only one individual gold medal on the track, the 400 metres, but they were successful in five of the field events, with thirteen medals out of a possible twenty-four, and both the relays.

The United States could not compare, however, with the impact made by the Finns who won all the track events from 1,500 metres upwards, including nine out of twelve medals, and the javelin and decathlon. The great Nurmi was beaten by his fellow countryman, Ville Ritola, in the 5,000 metres but he had defeated Ritola in the 10,000 metres. Nurmi came second in the steeplechase final after having, in his preliminary heat, fallen at the water-jump and damaged his precious stop-watch. In what proved to be his last Olympics, the peerless Finn had brought his total to nine gold and three silver medals.

Los Angeles, 1932

The New World hosts completely made up for the excesses of St Louis in 1904. Fine if dry Californian weather and superb facilities, including the 105,000 capacity Los Angeles Colosseum and the first Olympic Village (for men only, the women staying in hotels), produced some marvellous athletics.

As a fitting celebration of the return of the Olympics to the United States, the double sprint winner was the black American, Eddie Tolan. In the 100 metres the new photo-finish equipment had to be studied before Tolan was declared the winner by inches from his fellow American, Ralph Metcalfe. In the 200 metres the luckless Metcalfe was the victim of a miscalculation – his lane was too long by 1·50 m – and Tolan streaked ahead for his second victory.

Another thrilling American battle came in the 400 metres, in which Bill Carr pulled past his great rival, Ben Eastman, to set an astonishing world record of 46·2 sec. The bespectacled Tommy Hampson retained the 800 metres title for Britain; a keen believer in steady pace, Hampson had a first lap of 54·8 sec., followed by 54·9 sec. in the second, for a total time of 1 min. 49·7 sec., and became the first man to beat 1 min. 50 sec.

Controversy arose in the 5,000 metres when the Finn, Lauri Lehtinen, swung wide in the final straight, cutting off the American Ralph Hill. He was soundly booed by the crowd, but the announcer calmed them: 'Please remember these people are our guests.'

The 3,000 metres steeplechase came close to farce with an official's error causing the athletes to run an extra lap. But no one could doubt that Finland's Volmari Iso-Hollo deserved his victory. As well as the 800 metres, Britain won the 50,000 metres walk – thirty-nine-year-old Tommy Green finished nearly seven minutes ahead of his nearest rival. The Americans won their traditional victories in the high jump, long jump and pole vault, but the triple jump went to Chuhei Nambu of Japan, a country whose athletics had been greatly stimulated by the growth of the Olympic movement.

The first great international woman athlete was Kinoue Hitomi of Japan, who died in 1931. But it was not until 1932, in the Los Angeles Olympics that the women champions were given much publicity. In the 100 metres the winner was the powerful Stanislawa Walasiewicz of Poland, later to become an American citizen as Stella Walsh. Her top-class career was to continue until 1951, when she won her eleventh and last U S title in the long jump.

But the most celebrated woman athlete at Los Angeles was the Texas-born Mildred (Babe) Didrickson who, at eighteen, won the javelin and the 80 metres hurdles in world record time. She would also have finished first in the high jump, with a clearance of 1·67 m, but the judges decided that she had been jumping all afternoon with an illegal diving style and would therefore be placed second. Not until 1939 were the rules, which had led to this lightning judgement, changed. Babe Didrickson, who later married an American wrestler named Zaharias, was to make another reputation for herself as the world's top woman golfer.

Berlin, 1936

These Games are now invariably associated with the rise of the Nazi party in Germany, for although the International Olympic Committee tried hard to prevent it, the Berlin Games were used by Adolf Hitler as propaganda for the Nazis. Nevertheless, the arena was superb, the athletics events were outstanding, and Olympic and even world records were shattered.

The brilliant official film of those Games, directed by Leni Riefenstahl, was to do an immense service for the sport of athletics with its dramatic presentation of the field events as well as the more popular track races. It showed that champions like the American high jumper Cornelius Johnson, Japan's Naoto Tajima, the first triple jumper to beat 16 m, and the handsome American decathlon winner Glenn Morris deserved the spotlight just as much, say, as Kitei Son, the Korean marathon winner running in the colours of his country's conquerors, Japan.

For many observers the most exciting victory of all was that of New Zealand's Jack Lovelock, a student at Oxford University, in the 1,500 metres, with a world-record time of 3 min. 47·8 sec. Lovelock's winning burst from about 300 metres before the finish was perfectly judged. But Britain was also delighted with Harold Whitlock's margin of almost 1½ min. in the 50,000 metres walk, and a team victory in the 4 × 400 metres relay, anchored by Godfrey Brown.

The Germans, who had been in a special training camp for many weeks, won the shot, hammer and javelin, getting five out of the nine medals available in these three events. Though the German women won seven out of eighteen medals, they suffered a crushing disappointment, in front of Hitler himself, in the 4 × 100 metres relay, when they dropped the baton on the last exchange.

The American Helen Stephens was far out on her own in

the women's 100 metres, which she won in 11·5 sec. – half a second faster than the winning men's time in Athens in 1896. But there could be no doubt at all as to who was the champion of all champions at Berlin.

Jesse Owens, a black American from Cleveland, Ohio, had already astounded the athletics world with six world records within seventy minutes on 25 May 1935. Under the infinitely greater pressure of Olympic competition, he won the 100 metres in the wind-assisted – but still Olympic-record – time of 10·3 sec., the 200 metres in 20·7 sec., a world's best time round a full turn, and the long jump with 8·06 m. He also ran the last, anchor, stage for the winning American team in the 4×100 metres relay.

Owens's elegance in action, his coolness under stress, and his sportsmanship, as much as his four gold medals, were the highlight of the fine performance of the athletes at Berlin.

London, 1948

Austerity, after the war years of 1939–45, seemed likely to be the keynote of the Wembley Olympics. But Britain, in spite of a lack of any real athletic talent of its own at that time, made sure that the war-weary Europeans and the rest of the world were given a warm welcome.

Emil Zatopek of Czechoslovakia, winner of the 10,000 metres and second in the 5,000 metres, was one of the most colourful characters of the Games with his head-rolling, shoulder-shrugging style and keen sense of humour. Years later, when I met Zatopek in Prague, he told me: 'The Olympics in London, after all the killing and starvation of the war, was like the sun coming out, a liberation of the human spirit.'

One of the most unforgettable races on the Wembley track was the 400 metres with a dramatic struggle between two Jamaicans, Herb McKenley and Arthur Wint.

The smaller McKenley, labelled as 'the surest sure thing of the Games', went off so fast that he covered his first 200 metres far ahead of the giant-striding but seemingly leisurely Wint. But as McKenley was to recall: 'About half-way down the home straight it seemed that the entire stadium had fallen on me.' While McKenley struggled, Wint moved steadily past him to win in 46·2 sec., equalling Bill Carr's time at Los Angeles in 1932.

The biggest surprise came in the 100 metres, won by the American Harrison Dillard, who had been the clear favourite for the 110 metres hurdles until he had fallen in the final American trials. At the time Dillard had remarked, 'I can run some, too' and so it proved. At the end of the Games, Dillard gained a second gold medal in the sprint relay after the Americans had first been disqualified and then rein-stated. Four years later, in Helsinki, Dillard was to win in his real speciality, the high hurdles.

Other Wembley winners included Bob Mathias of the United States in the decathlon. He was only seventeen and had never before that year competed in the testing ten events. No wonder that at the finish he protested to his proud father 'No more decathlon, Dad, ever again.' Yet he was to retain his Olympic title in Helsinki four years later. The marathon saw three men on the final lap of the stadium at the same time before Argentina's Alfredo Cabrera, followed by Britain's Tom Richards, passed the flagging Belgian leader, Etienne Gailly.

The Dutch housewife and mother, Fanny Blankers-Koen, was in unbeatable form, winning four gold medals: the 100 and 200 metres, as well as the 80 metres hurdles and the sprint relay. Her popularity did much to boost women's athletics in Britain.

Helsinki, 1952

Track and field athletics are more popular in Finland than in any other country and so it was not surprising that the Helsinki Games were perfectly organized, with the jumps and throws receiving as much appreciation as the track races.

World records were beaten in the men's 4×400 metres relay, triple jump, hammer and decathlon, the women's 100 and 200 metres, 4×100 metres relay, 80 metres hurdles and shot, while the world's best performances (there were no official world records in these events at the time) were achieved in the men's steeplechase and 50,000 metres walk.

The USSR made its first entry in the Olympics in 1952 and although their team, as if cautious about close contact with the west, stayed in a 'village' of its own, their athletes made their mark. In the men's events they gained six medals and their women won eleven medals in nine events, with Aleksandra Chudina, third in the high jump and second in both the long jump and javelin, the best all-rounder.

Of the sixty countries which took part in the Olympic Games, by far the most successful was the United States with fourteen victories by the American men, and a gold for the women's sprint relay team which included Barbara Jones, aged only fifteen.

Herb McKenley had been frustrated in 1948 by losing the 400 metres to Arthur Wint but also by missing a team gold medal in the 4×400 metres relay – Wint had broken down with cramp. In Helsinki, McKenley, known as 'Hustling Herb', lost the 100 metres on a photo-finish and then was beaten in the 400 metres by another Jamaican, George Rhoden. But on the third stage of the 4×400 metres relay, Herb contributed a fantastic leg of 44·6 sec. which allowed Jamaica to win by just a stride from the Americans and gave McKenley the gold medal he so richly deserved.

The brightest star of the Games was Emil Zatopek. The Czechoslovak runner won the impossible treble of 5,000 metres, plus a heat, the 10,000 metres and then, in his first ever attempt at the longest Olympic run, the marathon. Emil's wife Dana brought the couple's total to four gold medals with her victory in the javelin.

Two unexpected winners were Horace Ashenfelter of the United States in the steeplechase, having previously ranked only seventeenth in the world, and little Josy Barthel of Luxembourg in the 1,500 metres. No wonder Barthel wept for joy on the victory rostrum as they played his country's national anthem. And the Australian sprinter Marjorie Jackson, having won the 100 and 200 metres, both in world-record time, could be excused a tear when the relay baton was knocked from her grasp by an incoming team-mate's knee.

Melbourne, 1956

It was remarkable that these Games were held at all considering the various political upheavals around the world at that time. But held they were amidst a friendly atmosphere, even though some of the athletics facilities did not reach the same high standard as in Helsinki.

Russia's distance runner Vladimir Kuts and the American sprinter Bobby Joe Morrow headed the list of champions. The United States took fifteen men's titles out of twenty-four. Kuts crushed the British hope, Gordon Pirie, after a battle lasting for twenty-one of the twenty-five laps of the 10,000 metres; he also destroyed the opposition in the 5,000 metres. Morrow came through powerfully in the 100 metres for a clear victory against the wind, and followed this with a sweeping run in the 200 metres and a third gold in the sprint relay.

Britain's only gold – they had not won one in 1948 or 1952 – came in the steeplechase, where Chris Brasher was at first disqualified for obstruction, but was later reinstated. In the 800 metres Derek Johnson came close to victory, only to be beaten in the last few strides by the American Tom Courtney.

The 1,500 metres went unpredictably to the high-stepping Ron Delany of Ireland, thanks to a sprint of just 25·6 sec. over the last 200 metres. Alain Mimoun of France won the marathon, with the gallant Emil Zatopek, still recovering from an illness, finishing sixth.

The field events produced two new world records, a woman's high jump of 1·76 m by the American Mildred McDaniel and a mighty men's javelin throw of 85·71 m by Norway's Egil Danielsen – the javelin sailed across the centre of the Melbourne Cricket Ground and landed near the pole vault. The American men won the three other throws, shot, discus and hammer, and three out of the four jumps, while Russian women took the javelin and shot.

The happiest sight for the Melbourne crowd was Australia's seventeen-year-old Betty Cuthbert, mouth wide open as if gasping for air, winning the 100 and 200 metres and then anchoring her sprint relay team for yet another win in world-record time. 'Betty, You Beaut', ran a typically Australian newspaper headline the next day.

Rome, 1960

Germany gained its first ever Olympic track victory through the fast-starting 100 metres specialist Armin Hary. The United States also failed to retain the 200 metres which, to the huge delight of the crowd, went to the smooth-striding Italian Livio Berruti. A virtually unknown Ethiopian, Abebe Bikila, won the marathon in bare feet. For the first time, European runners failed to win the 5,000 metres, thanks to the courageous breakaway tactics of New Zealand's Murray Halberg; his fellow Kiwi, Peter Snell, was the victor over 800 metres on the same afternoon.

Britain suffered many disappointments, for her only gold medal was won by Don Thompson, who had prepared thoroughly for the Roman heat, in the 50,000 metres walk.

The Olympic champions were now coming from a far wider range of countries than ever before. For the first time the International Amateur Athletic Federation stated that each country should be allowed one entry per event by right, and that for more entries, up to the maximum of three, the competitors must have achieved official qualifying standards (laid down by the IAAF) between October 1959 and August 1960.

On the track, the high point at Rome came on 6 September in the finals of the men's 400 and 1,500 metres. The 400 metres produced an unforgettable protracted struggle between Carl Kaufmann of Germany and the American Otis Davis. Kaufmann led narrowly at two hundred metres but then Davis accelerated in the third hundred metres and entered the long home straight with a clear lead. The gold medal seemed to be his, but Kaufmann fought back until he was level with Davis's shoulder as they crossed the line. Davis had just won, and the time, 44·9 sec., was a new world record.

There was only one outstanding runner in the 1,500 metres, the Australian, Herb Elliott, who had never yet suffered defeat over this distance or the mile. Elliott did not really come into the picture until the penultimate back straight. Then he pulled away, covering the last 800 metres in 1 min. 52·8 sec. and winning unchallenged in 3 min. 35·6 sec. 0·4 sec. faster than his own world record.

The biggest upset in the men's field events was the defeat of the American world-record-holder, John Thomas, in the high jump by the Russian, Robert Shavlakadze and his eighteen-year-old team-mate, Valeriy Brumel, who took the silver medal. The United States won both the long jump and the pole vault and shared the four throws with the Soviet Union. Rafer Johnson won an absorbing decathlon from Yang Chuan Kwang, who, though representing Taiwan, had been a fellow student of Johnson's at the University of California.

The leading woman athlete was the black American Wilma Rudolph, aged nineteen. She was the seventeenth child in a family of nineteen, and claimed 'I learned to run fast because I wanted to get to that dining table first.' An indifferent starter, Wilma was a dazzling sight in full stride as she won both the 100 and 200 metres. (Britain's Dorothy Hyman took the silver and bronze medals in these events.) Wilma Rudolph took a third gold in the sprint relay. Most of the women's athletics programme was dominated by the Russians, including the 800 metres, which was revived for the first time since 1928.

Tokyo, 1964

This was by far Britain's greatest Olympics. There were gold medals in the men's (Lynn Davies) and women's (Mary Rand) long jump, the 20,000 metres walk (Ken Matthews) and the women's 800 metres (Ann Packer), and silver medals in seven other events.

The Tokyo Olympics provided first-class facilities and the

competitors responded with enthusiasm. Arguably the greatest 100 metres sprinter ever seen, was the heavily built American Bob Hayes who, on the last leg of the sprint relay – moving the United States from third to first place – certainly surpassed 26·5 miles per hour as he hurled himself forward with the force of a clenched fist.

The king of the middle distances was New Zealand's Peter Snell who not only retained his 800 metres crown but also took the 1,500 metres, the first time this double had been accomplished since 1920, when competition had been far less demanding. The big-chested Snell completely dominated the opposition.

Americans most surprisingly won both the 5,000 and 10,000 metres as well as their usual specialities like the 110 and 400 metres hurdles, pole vault, shot and both relays. In the discus, Al Oerter retained the title he had won both in 1956 and 1960 and was to win yet again in 1968. Abebe Bikila kept the marathon for Ethiopia in a world's best performance of 2 hr 12 min. 11·2 sec.

The gold medals in the women's athletics were spread fairly widely among the various countries, although the Russian sisters Tamara and Irina Press collected three between them. But few would disagree that the greatest single effort was Mary Rand's world-record long jump of 6·76 m. She also came second in the pentathlon and completed her set of Olympic medals for Britain with a bronze in the 4 × 100 metres relay.

Mexico City, 1968

No Olympic meeting, as far as athletics was concerned, was attended by more controversy beforehand than the Mexico

Games. The major problem was the high altitude of Mexico City – over 2,134 m above sea level – which meant that no middle- or long-distance runner from a low-altitude country had any real chance of beating the 'men of the mountains'. Australia's Ron Clarke, for example, went to Mexico as a multiple record-breaker but came close to collapse during the final stages of the 10,000 metres and had to be revived afterwards with an oxygen mask.

On the other hand, the thin air was an advantage in the 'explosive' events like the short sprints and hurdles and the long and triple jumps.

It would be ungenerous, however, to deny the success of African athletes in Mexico even though many of them had benefited from having lived or trained at high altitude. Kipchoge Keino of Kenya, for example, ran in the 10,000, 5,000 and 1,500 metres and his winning time of 3 min. 34·9 sec. in the 1,500 metres was certainly worth better than the then world record, set at low altitude, of 3 min. 33·1 sec.

But the choice of Mexico City for the 1968 Games meant that, to give themselves a fair chance, many of the athletes had to sacrifice even more of their time to allow for special high-altitude training. One could no longer, it seemed, afford to be a part-timer in sport.

Britain's one gold medal in the athletics earned international respect. It was won by David Hemery, an Englishman who had lived and studied in the United States as much as in Britain. Attacking from the very start, he won the 400 metres hurdles in 48·1 sec., a world record by 0·7 sec., with the rest of the field left flagging far behind.

Even more incredible was the feat of the American Bob Beamon in the long jump. Aided by a following wind of exactly two metres per second (the maximum permissible for records) plus low atmospheric pressure and air density, Beamon improved the world record from 8·34 m to 8·90 m with one enormous leap. No wonder that Beamon himself, overwhelmed by a jump which may remain unequalled this century, fell to his knees weeping with shock.

The old-timer Al Oerter won his fourth successive Olympic discus title for the United States and received even more praise than the smooth sprint victories of Jim Hines (100 metres) and Tommie Smith (200 metres).

The field events also included a new world record of 17·39 m by the Russian Viktor Saneyev, and the arrival of a notable innovator in the high jump. To the incredulity of most of the crowd, Dick Fosbury of the USA adopted a fast, curving run towards the high jump bar and then turned at the last minute to clear the bar backwards with his legs flipping upwards. The technique was promptly nicknamed the 'Fosbury flop' and has been known by this name ever since.

The first 100 metres sprinter ever to retain the Olympic title was the American, Wyomia Tyus, who had won the women's event in Tokyo and now set a world record of 11 sec. Athletes from eastern Europe won all three women's throws and the high and long jumps.

The women's 400 metres produced a thrilling finish between Britain's Lillian Board, one of the favourites for the title, and the 'dark horse', the French girl, Colette Besson. Lillian, a bubbling, friendly girl who was to die of cancer when she was only twenty-two, was just passed by Colette Besson on the line. However, she had the considerable consolation of winning two gold medals in the European Championships in the following year.

Munich, 1972

The death of eleven Israeli competitors and officials, after they had been held to hostage by Palestinian terrorists in the Olympic Village itself, overshadowed the Munich Games. Indeed, some critics, though not the remaining members of the Israeli team, suggested that the Munich Olympics should be abandoned. Others felt that the Olympic movement, dedicated to peace, should not be seen to give way to political extremists.

In spite of this shadow some remarkable champions were to dominate the Munich Olympics. Valeriy Borzov of the Soviet Union won both the sprints, showing superb technique and coolness as well as speed. No Americans competed in the 100 metres because the three United States athletes, through a misunderstanding about the timetable, arrived at the stadium too late for the second round of the event.

Another accident came close to frustrating the gold-medal hopes of Lasse Viren of Finland: just before the half-way mark in the 10,000 metres Gammoudi of Tunisia slipped and fell, causing Viren to tumble, too. Although he had lost more than two seconds on the leaders, Viren somehow recovered to such effect that he pulled away powerfully in the last 600 m and won in world-record time. Later he also won the 5,000 metres, reviving memories of the dominance of the Finnish runners in the 1920s and 1930s.

As well as the mix-up over the men's 100 metres, the usnally powerful United States suffered other disappointments. In the 1,500 metres their world-record-holder, Jim Ryun, fell in his heat and failed to quality. For the first time since 1896, the Americans did not win the pole vault, the winner being Wolfgang Nordwig of East Germany, and they also failed to retain the titles in the discus and high jump. But the fast-finishing Dave Wottle, wearing a lucky golf cap, took the 800 metres for the United States by three hundredths of a second and Frank Shorter was a clear winner of the marathon.

David Hemery of Britain, in spite of a characteristically determined effort, lost his 400 metres hurdles title to John Akii-Bua from Uganda. Akii-Bua achieved a new world-record time, showing that Africa could produce hurdlers as well as middle- and long-distance runners.

Britain's only gold medal was won by thirty-three-year-old Mary Peters who had trained for the event in Belfast, despite the Irish troubles, and won the pentathlon with a world-record score. Second was West Germany's Heide Rosendahl, who won the long jump and took a second gold medal in the 4×100 metres relay. Germany also won the women's high jump – through the sixteen-year-old Ulrike Meyforth – and the men's javelin. But East Germany won an enviable twelve medals, six of them gold, from the fourteen women's athletics events in Munich.

Montreal, 1976

The biggest blow to the Canadian organizers, as the Olympics crossed the Atlantic to the North American continent for the first time since 1932, was a last-minute mass withdrawal of the black African countries. The black boycott was in protest at continuing New Zealand rugby football contacts with South Africa, the land of apartheid, and the failure, in the Africans' eyes, of the International Olympic Committee to criticize such contacts strongly enough.

Athletics was affected by the boycott more than any other Olympic sport. One notable absentee, for example, was the 400 metres hurdler Akii-Bua of Uganda, who was unable to defend the title he had won so dramatically four years before. His successor as Olympic champion and world-record-holder, a black American named Edwin Moses, spoke for many other Olympians when he said of the African boycott: 'I very much regret it. The Games are there to bring together the best athletes in the world.'

Probably the best athlete taking part at Montreal was Alberto Juantorena of Cuba. First he won the 800 metres in world-record time, though it was only his ninth race at the distance. Four days later he took the 400 metres in 44·26 sec., the fastest time ever achieved away from the helpfully thin air of high altitudes. In the 4×400 metres relay, running the last leg for Cuba, the huge-striding, muscular Juantorena went all out, covering the first 200 metres in 20·1 sec. before he realized he was only human and was forced to finish in a 'mere' 44·7 sec.

Lasse Viren of Finland was almost as impressive, retaining both the 5,000 and 10,000 metres titles he had won in Munich and also coming fifth in the marathon, which was won by Waldemar Cierpinski, a former East German steeplechaser. Viren, who had shown indifferent form between Munich and Montreal, proved again that he was the master when it mattered most. He said later: 'I run because of curiosity and ambition. I want to see what my limits are. A runner is never satisfied.'

The supreme all-rounder at Montreal was the American Bruce Jenner, winner of the two-day decathlon with a world-record score of 8,618 points. Remarkably versatile, he had a winning margin of more than 200 points at the end of the 1,500 metres, which he covered almost as though it was a three-and-a-half-lap lap of honour.

Outstanding in the field events were Miklos Nemeth of Hungary in the javelin and Viktor Saneyev from the Soviet Union in the triple jump. With his opening throw Nemeth, whose father Imre had been Olympic hammer champion back in 1948, sent the javelin sailing out to a world-record distance of 94·58 m, thus disproving those critics who had claimed he was never at his best on a big occasion. The margin of Nemeth's victory, 6·66 m, was the widest in the history of the Olympic field events.

As for triple jumper Saneyev, he won his third successive Olympic title in spite of frequent leg injuries. He later admitted, 'A whole week after Montreal I couldn't sleep well. I was so excited it was just like winning the gold medal for the first time.'

The outstanding woman champion was also the shortest and lightest competitor at 1·62 m and 47·2 kg. Tatyana Kazankina from the Soviet Union first took the 800 metres in the world-record time of 1 min. 54·9 sec., and then, with a powerful last lap, the 1,500 metres. But even the normally restrained observers in the Press Box applauded the victory of Poland's Irena Szewinska in the 400 metres in world-record time. It was, after all, her fourth Olympics and she had always been friendly and unspoiled.

Montreal, it must be said, was not particularly successful for British athletes. The only medal to be won was a bronze by Brendan Foster in the 10,000 metres. But by now, eighty-four years after the first modern Olympics, it is obvious that the whole world has learned how to run, jump and throw to the highest standards.

3   The Commonwealth Games, the European Championships and the European Cup

The Commonwealth Games

Although the idea was first suggested in 1891, the British Empire Games, as they were then called, did not come into being until 1930, at Hamilton in Canada. They have since been staged in London (1934), Sydney (1938), Auckland (1950), Vancouver (1954), Cardiff (1958), Perth, Australia (1962), Kingston, Jamaica (1966), Edinburgh (1970), Christchurch, New Zealand (1974) and Edmonton, Canada (1978). The next Commonwealth Games will be held at Brisbane in 1982.

Athletics has always been the centrepiece of these multi-sport Games which switched from yards to metres in 1970. Amongst the most memorable days in the history of the Games was that at Vancouver when England's marathon runner Jim Peters collapsed on the final circuit of the track and the race went to Joe McGhee of Scotland. On the same sultry afternoon England's Roger Bannister strode past John Landy of Australia to win the battle between the first two men to run a mile in less than four minutes.

In 1974 in Christchurch, spear-heading some remarkable African running, Filbert Bayi of Tanzania led from gun to tape to win the 1,500 metres in world-record time.

Freakish wind and temperature changes affected many of the athletic performances in Edmonton in 1978 but Kenya's Henry Rono was supreme in the 5,000 metres and steeplechase and England's Daley Thompson, just a week past his twentieth birthday, won the decathlon with the third highest ever points score for the two-day event. Overall, England won sixteen gold medals, Australia and Canada six each, Kenya five and Scotland two. The most unexpected winner of all was the Tanzanian marathon runner Gidemas Shahanga who cut seven minutes off his personal best time. The outstanding woman champion was Diane Konihowski in the pentathlon but the English girls had their first-ever clean sweep since 1934 when Lorna Boothe won the 100 metres hurdles ahead of Shirley Strong and Sharon Colyear.

The European Championships

The first European Championships, held in Turin in 1934, were not supported by Britain as British athletics organizers had not at that time accepted the idea of the season continuing into the late summer months. Subsequent European Championships were celebrated in Paris (1938), Oslo (1946), Brussels (1950), Berne (1954), Stockholm (1958), Belgrade (1962), Budapest (1966), Athens (1969), Helsinki (1971), Rome (1974) and Prague (1978).

The highpoints of the early Championships must include the 5,000 and 10,000 metres double of Czechoslovakia's Emil Zatopek in 1950, the extraordinary breakthrough of the Russian Vladimir Kuts (Zatopek's successor in the long distances) in 1954, and the remarkable all-round effort of Britain's team in 1958, including victories in the 400 metres (John Wrighton), 800 metres (Michael Rawson), 1,500 metres (Brian Hewson), 4×400 metres relay, shot (Arthur Rowe), 20,000 metres walk (Stan Vickers) and women's 100 metres (Heather Young).

The Soviet Union dominated the 1962 meeting in Belgrade

with seven men's titles and six gold medals in the women's events, while Britain won the 400 metres (Robbie Brightwell), 5,000 metres (Bruce Tulloh), marathon (Brian Kilby), 20,000 metres walk (Ken Matthews) and women's 100 metres (Dorothy Hyman).

Four years later in Budapest, East Germany – or the German Democratic Republic to give it the proper name – made its first appearance in the Championships as a separate team (they had hitherto combined with West Germany – the German Federal Republic). The East Germans celebrated by winning a total of seventeen medals – eight of them gold. Britain's two titles, and only medals of any kind, came through Lynn Davies (long jump) and Jim Hogan (marathon).

The Championships were growing steadily in public appeal but they were fortunate to survive the shock at Athens in 1969 when the West German team withdrew at the last minute from all the events except the relays. This was a spontaneous act of protest by the athletes themselves after it had been ruled, correctly, that Jurgen May, a defector from East Germany, was not eligible to represent them in the 1,500 metres because he had not lived in his new country for three years. East Germany won twenty-five medals, one more than the Soviet Union. Britain's total of seventeen medals included victories in the 1,500 metres (John Whetton), 5,000 metres (Ian Stewart), marathon (Ron Hill), 20,000 metres walk (Paul Nihill), women's 800 metres (Lillian Board) and the women's 4×400 metres relay in which Lillian ran a perfectly judged final leg.

The return of the Championships to Helsinki in 1971 was, for many athletics purists, the perfect move, for in no other country in the world is track and field as highly regarded as it is in Finland. The hosts gained their reward for superb organization in the magnificent long-distance double victory of their own Juha Vaatainen over the 10,000 metres and the

5,000 metres. Britain's David Bedford, sadly finding that he lacked sufficient strength to break away from the faster finishers early on, was sixth in the 10,000 metres.

Indeed, Britain's only gold medal of the Championships came from the nineteen-year-old David Jenkins in the 400 metres, which he won in the outside lane. By contrast, the East Germans swept to triumph, winning a total of thirty-two medals, twelve of them gold. The Soviet Union, though its population was twenty times greater than that of East Germany, had a total medal count of twenty, including seven men's titles.

A revision of the international athletics calendar meant that the European Championships of 1971 in Helsinki were followed by the Championships in Rome in 1974. Britain had four victories: Alan Pascoe (400 metres hurdles), Brendan Foster (5,000 metres), Ian Thompson (marathon) and the 4×400 metres relay team of Glen Cohen, Bill Hartley, Alan Pascoe and David Jenkins.

The East Germans won four men's events, including the 1,500 and 10,000 metres, and six women's gold medals; the Russians had won six men's events and three women's. Poland took both the steeplechase and the decathlon and had arguably the greatest athlete of the Championships in Irena Szewinska, winner of the women's 100 and 200 metres. She also sprinted outstandingly in both relay finals.

Rome had been hot and sultry throughout the competition. At Prague in 1978 the European Championships were conducted in chilly and often wet weather. Britain's only winner was Steve Ovett, unconquerable in the 1,500 metres after earlier finishing second in the 800 metres behind East Germany's unheralded Olaf Beyer. Not for the first time Britain found it very hard to compete at top level in the European Championships, especially when they came so soon after the Commonwealth Games. The highest praise should go to Daley Thompson who was second in the gruelling decathlon, finishing only 51 points behind the Russian Aleksandr Grebenyuk.

Possibly the outstanding competitor in the men's events in Prague was the Italian sprinter, Pietro Mennea, who won both the 100 and 200 metres and, in his tenth run of the meeting, contributed a 44·2 sec. 'leg' in the 4×400 metres relay. Martti Vainio of Finland in the 10,000 metres and the Russian high jumper Vladimir Yashchenko were also very impressive.

The best women champions refused to be dispirited by the weather and set world records in the 400 metres, 400 metres hurdles, high jump and long jump. In the javelin, runner-up Tessa Sanderson became the first British woman to win a European championship medal in any of the throws and the British sprint relay team finished second.

Not many weeks after the athletes had left Prague came the disturbing news that five of them, four from the Soviet Union, had been disqualified for failing drug tests. They included Nadyezhda Tkachenko, the winner of the women's pentathlon in Prague, and Yevgeniy Mironov, who had taken the silver medal in the men's shot.

The European Cup

The nearest that athletics, basically such an individualistic sport, comes to team competition is the European Cup, launched in 1965. Each country enters one athlete per event. Points are awarded on the basis of six to the first competitor, five to the second and so on down to one point for sixth place. A preliminary round is followed by semi-finals and then the finals. The present system is by no means perfect – some commentators feel that many of the track races would be more exciting with two competitors per country – but it has produced some memorable moments including the final in Turin in 1979.

Here are the team winners for each Cup final, with Britain's position.

MEN: 1965, Soviet Union (Britain 6th); 1967, Soviet Union (Britain did not qualify); 1970, East Germany (Britain did not qualify); 1973, Soviet Union (Britain 4th); 1975, East Germany (Britain 4th); 1977, East Germany (Britain 4th); 1979, East Germany (Britain 5th).

WOMEN: 1965, Soviet Union (Britain did not qualify); 1967, Soviet Union (Britain 5th); 1970, East Germany (Britain 5th); 1973, East Germany (Britain 4th equal); 1975, East Germany (Britain 7th); 1977, East Germany (Britain 3rd); 1979, East Germany (Britain 4th).

The World Cup

The first World Cup was held in Dusseldorf in 1977, a Europe Select team winning the women's competition and East Germany the men's trophy. In Montreal two years later East Germany took the women's cup and the United States, the men's.

4 Great Athletes, Past and Present

Ackermann, Rosemarie (East Germany), high jumper, born 1952. Olympic champion in 1976. 1·75 m tall; uses the straddle style. The first woman to clear 2 m – 25 cm higher than her own head – which she did in 1977. A superbly cool-headed competitor.

Akii-Bua, John (Uganda), 400 metres hurdler, born 1949. The Olympic champion at Munich in 1972, when his vigorous sense of attack over the hurdles brought him to a surprising world record time of 47·82 sec. This was proof that Africa could produce athletes of the top class in technical events as well as middle- and long-distance running.

Bannister Roger (Britain), miler, born 1929. The first man to beat the four-minute 'barrier' for the mile on 6 May 1954, at Oxford, with a time of 3 min. 59·4 sec. In a short but extraordinarily successful athletics career, Bannister, who was later to make his mark in medicine and be knighted by the Queen, was also Commonwealth Games mile and European 1,500 metres champion thanks to his powerful finish over the last 300 m.

Bardauskiene, Vilma (Soviet Union), long jumper, born 1953. A fine sprinter, she came to the top in the 1978 season with a world record of 7·07 m which she improved to 7·09 m during the European Championships in Prague. Strong and fast, she was coached by the former Russian men's world-record-holder Igor Ter-Ovanesyan.

Bayi, Filbert (Tanzania), 1,500 metres runner, born 1953. Made his greatest impact by winning the 1974 Commonwealth Games 1,500 metres in the world-record time of 3 min. 32·2 sec., having led from gun to tape against a strong field. Like the Ugandan hurdler Akii-Bua, Bayi was unable to compete in the 1976 Olympics because of the mass African withdrawal from the Games.

Beamon, Bob (United States), long jumper, born 1946. The Olympic champion of 1968 in Mexico, with the almost unbelievable world-record long jump of 8·90 m, which surpassed the previous record by 55 cm. Some observers felt that the following wind was really stronger than two metres per second (the limit for records) but none the less Beamon, undoubtedly aided by the thin atmosphere at high altitude, used his speed (9·4 sec. for 100 yards) and spring to the maximum advantage. Most experts believe that Beamon's world record may not be beaten for at least another ten years.

Bedford, David (Britain), 10,000 metres runner, born 1949. At only nineteen he set his first national record with 28 min. 24·4 sec. for 10,000 metres in 1969. Four years later, at the AAA Championships at Crystal Palace he cut 7·6 sec. from the then world record with a time of 27 min. 30·8 sec. At his best a great front runner, he was destined never to win a major track title in either the European Championships or Olympic Games and eventually became handicapped by a persistent leg injury.

Beyer, Udo (East Germany), shot putter, born 1955. The Olympic champion of 1976 and the European title winner of 1978, he set a world record of 22·15 m in 1978, though this was still well behind the 22·86 m, three years earlier by the American Brian Oldfield, who was then a professional and therefore could not have his distance ratified by the governing bodies of amateur athletics. Just 1·94 m tall, Beyer proved an outstanding competitor after his unexpected victory in the 1976 Olympics.

Bikila, Abebe (Ethiopia), marathon runner, born 1932. The only man to have retained the Olympic marathon title, he won in Rome in 1960 in 2 hr 15 min. 16·2 sec. and in Tokyo in 1964 in 2 hr. 12 min. 11·2 sec. Both were world's best performances, the first being achieved in bare feet after regular training at high altitude in his own country. Bikila received serious spinal injuries in a car crash in 1969, became paralysed from the waist down and died in 1973, aged forty-one.

Blankers-Koen, Fanny (Holland), all-round athlete, born 1918. At the 1948 Olympics in London she won the 100 and 200 metres and the 80 metres hurdles, and anchored the Dutch team to victory in the 4 × 100 metres relay. Five times champion of Europe, she beat or equalled eleven world records, ranging from the 100 yards in 1938 to the pentathlon in 1951.

Borzov, Valeriy (Soviet Union), sprinter, born 1949. Already three times a European sprint champion, he won both the 100 and 200 metres at the Olympics of 1972 in Munich – the first European ever to achieve the double in these events. Often described as a man-made sprinter, he had nerves of steel and a marvellous innate sense of relaxation even at top speed.

Brumel, Valeriy (Soviet Union), high jumper, born 1942. Second, at only eighteen, in the 1960 Olympics in Rome, he won the gold medal at Tokyo four years later and, between 1961 and 1963, beat the world record six times, using the straddle technique, with a best-ever performance of 2·28 m. Although he was seriously injured in 1965 in a road accident, he returned to competition after 1,000 days in hospital and six operations, and cleared 2·06 m.

Capes, Geoffrey (Britain), shot putter, born 1949. Commonwealth Games champion for England in 1974 and 1978 and twice European champion, he has represented his country more than sixty times since 1976 and held the British record at 21·55 m. A policeman, coached by BBC television commentator Stuart Storey, Capes has himself organized many training schemes for youngsters.

Clarke, Ron (Australia), distance runner, born 1937. A former junior mile record-holder, with 4 min. 6·8 sec. in 1956, the year that he carried the Olympic torch into the Melbourne arena, Clarke eventually set eighteen world records, including 13 min. 16·6 sec. for 5,000 metres and 27 min. 39·4 sec. for 10,000 metres without the benefit of the modern all-weather tracks. A remarkable front runner, he was destined never to win an Olympic title but he is regarded as an outstanding pioneer of the longer track events.

Coe, Sebastian (Britain), middle-distance runner, born 1956. First gained international recognition with third place in the European junior 1,500 metres in 1975. Two years later he won the European indoor title over 800 metres. The slim, lightly built Coe, whose poise and rhythm on the track began to hint at a remarkable future, took the world of athletics by storm during the summer of 1979. In Oslo he set a world 800 metres record of 1 min. 42·4 sec. and then a world-mile-record of 3 min. 49 sec. against a top-class field, before winning the European Cup 800 metres final with a blazing last 200 m. He completed a unique triple of world records in less than six weeks by running the 1,500 metres in 3 min. 32·1 sec. in Zurich on 15 August. Sebastian Coe's future could include breaking through 3 min. 30 sec. for 1,500 metres or a world record at 5,000 metres if he decides to increase his distance.

Davies, Lynn (Britain), long jumper, born in 1942. Unexpected but worthy winner of the Olympic title at Tokyo in 1964 with a leap of 8·07 m, the first time he had ever beaten 8 m. Davies later won the European title, was twice Commonwealth Games champion and has held the British record at 8·25 m since 1968. After retirement this versatile and highly intelligent Welsh athlete became director of coaching in Canada and then returned to manage British athletics teams.

Elliott, Herb (Australia), middle-distance runner, born in 1938. Between 1957 and 1963, in forty-three races over the mile or 1,500 metres, this utterly determined competitor was never beaten. At the Rome Olympics in 1960, Elliott, who had already lowered the world mile record to 3 min. 54·5 sec, ran right away from the opposition to set another world record of 3 min. 35·6 sec. for the 1,500 m. He is regarded by many people as the greatest miler of all time in spite of the claims of the American Jim Ryun.

Evans, Lee (United States), 400 metres runner, born 1947. Powerfully built and a determined competitor, he is the only man to have won four successive American titles at 400 metres. He won the Olympic gold medal at Mexico City in the world-record time of 43·8 sec.

Fosbury, Dick (United States), high jumper, born 1947. The 'Fosbury flop', the nickname for his jumping style, in which the competitor crosses the bar on his back, has now become part of the vocabulary of athletics. Fosbury started to experiment with his version of jumping in 1964 and four years later won the Olympic title in Mexico City with a leap of 2·24 m.

Foster, Brendan (Britain), distance runner, born 1948. As a 1,500 metres specialist Foster was an Olympic finalist in 1972. He first made his name internationally when he moved up distance with world records over two miles (8 min. 13·7 sec.) and 3,000 metres (7 min. 35·2 sec.) before a European record of 27 min. 30·3 sec. for 10,000 metres. In the 1976 Olympics, 'Big Bren', as he is hailed by his Gateshead supporters, finished third in the 10,000 metres, but his notable victories include the European 5,000 metres (1974) and three wins (two over 5,000 and one at 10,000 metres) in the European Cup final, as well as the Commonwealth Games 10,000 metres, and the English cross-country title over nine miles. No modern British distance runner has won more honours.

Fuchs, Ruth (East Germany), javelin thrower, born 1946. Winner of the Olympic titles both in 1972 and 1976, three times European champion, she set a new world record of 69·52 m in 1979 and is surely the most consistent champion in all the women's three throwing events. One of her rare defeats came from Britain's Tessa Sanderson in a European Cup semi-final.

George, Walter (Britain), middle and distance runner, born 1858. A man in advance of his time for, after an outstanding amateur career, which included records over distances of from one to six miles, George turned professional and in 1886 ran the mile in 4 min. 12¾ sec. This was not to be beaten for another twenty-nine years. In training, watched by a respected British reporter, George himself had earlier achieved the time of 4min. 10·2 sec. In his way, as much of a Grand Old Man of his sport as the cricketer, W. G. Grace.

Gohr, Marlies (East Germany), sprinter, born 1958. Formerly Marlies Oelsner. She was a finalist in the 1976 Montreal Olympic 100 metres and the following season became the first woman to beat 11 sec., on electric rather than hand-timing, with 10·88 sec.

Haegg, Gunder (Sweden), middle distance runner, born 1918. During the Second World War, when Sweden remained neutral, Haegg, stimulated by a keen rivalry with his fellow Swede Arne Andersson, lowered the world 1,500 metres record to 3 min. 43 sec. and the mile to 4 min. 1·4 sec. In his second-ever run over the distance Haegg became the first man to run 5,000 metres under 14 min. when, in 1942, he took 10·6 sec. off the previous world record with a time of 13 min. 58·2 sec. Both this and his mile record (the latter eventually beaten by Britain's Roger Bannister) were unsurpassed until 1954.

Harbig, Rudolf (Germany), middle-distance runner, born 1913. Remembered for his remarkable 800 metres world record of 1 min. 46·6 sec. in 1939, which was to remain unbeaten for another eighteen years. Harbig, who also equalled the world 400 metres record with 46 sec. in the same year, was killed on the Eastern Front in 1944. He was one of the first athletes to follow interval track training (see page 80).

Hayes, Bob (United States), sprinter, born 1942. Quite possibly the greatest of all athletes over 100 metres, judging from his final 'anchor' stage in the Olympic 4 × 100 metres relay at Tokyo in 1964 when, with a flying start, he covered his 100 m stage in the unofficial time of 8·6 sec. Hayes won the Olympic title in 10 sec. on a rain-soaked cinders track and won by the margin of 2 m. It will never be known how fast Bob Hayes could have run because, at only twenty-two, he left amateur athletics for American professional football.

Hemery, David (Britain), 400 metres hurdler, born 1944. He was born in Gloucestershire, but spent much of his boyhood in the United States. He first made his mark as junior A A A high hurdles champion over 120 yards and was high hurdles champion of the Commonwealth in 1966 and in 1970. He is best remembered for his 400 metres victory for an Olympic gold medal at Mexico City in 1968. Hemery attacked from the starting gun and won by the huge margin of 7 m, cutting 0·7 sec. off the previous world record with a time of 48·1 sec. Four years later, in Munich, Hemery took the bronze medal in the 400 metres hurdles (his time was 48·6 sec.) and completed his medal collection with a silver as a member of Britain's 4 × 400 metres relay team.

Hines, Jim (United States), sprinter, born 1946. The first man officially to beat 10 sec. for 100 metres, in the semi-final of the 1968 American championships, losing the final after a bad start. At the Mexico City Olympics, later the same year, Hines won the title clearly in 9·95 sec. (electrically timed), which was to survive as the world record for more than another ten years. The fact that all sprint races at these Olympics were helped by the thin air of high altitude does not detract from Hines's greatness as a sprinter.

Ibbotson, Derek (Britain), middle- and long-distance runner, born 1932. The bronze medal winner over 5,000 metres in the 1956 Olympics, Ibbotson moved down to the mile the following season and lowered the world record from 3 min. 58 sec. to 3 min. 57·2 sec. in an international race at London's White City stadium, in which the reigning Olympic 1,500 metres champion Ronnie Delany of Ireland was a distant second.

Jenkins, Dave (Britain) 4x400 metres relay;

Jenner, Bruce (United States), decathlete, born 1949. After much personal sacrifice, including training for nearly six hours a day, Jenner realized his great ambition by winning the Montreal Olympic decathlon with a world-record points score of 8,618. His personal records, when he retired after the Games, included 10·7 sec. (100 metres), 47·5 sec. (400 metres), 14·3 sec. (110 metres hurdles), 2.·03 m (high jump) and 7·32 m (long jump). His secret was that he worked technically on all of the ten events to make sure that he had no weaknesses in running, jumping or throwing.

Juantorena, Alberto (Cuba), middle-distance runner, born 1951. The first athlete to win both the Olympic 400 and 800 metres titles in the same Games, he achieved this magnificent double at Montreal in 1976 with times, respectively, of 44·26 sec. and 1 min. 43·5 sec. The latter was a world record, which Juantorena improved by 0·1 sec. in 1977. Tall (he had formerly been a basketball player), and with a giant stride, Juantorena also possessed a fiery competitive nature.

Kazankina, Tatyana (Soviet Union), middle-distance runner, born 1951. Early in 1976 she lowered the world 1,500 metres record to 3 min. 56 sec., the first woman to beat the 4 min. barrier. At Montreal, she won first the 800 metres in a world record time of 1 min. 54·9 sec. and then showed her versatility as a competitor by out-sprinting the field with a last lap of 56·9 sec. in the 1,500 metres.

Keino, Kipchoge (Kenya), middle-distance runner, born 1940. The first great African track racer, Keino beat the world 3,000 metres record with 7 min. 39·6 sec. in 1965 and the next year won both the 1,500 and the 5,000 metres in the Kingston (Jamaica) Commonwealth Games. At the Mexico City Olympics in 1968, he undoubtedly benefited from having trained at a high altitude in Kenya. He ran in both the 10,000 and 5,000 metres (where he was the runner-up) and then took the 1,500 metres gold medal in 3 min. 34·9 sec. After winning the 1970 Commonwealth 1,500 metres, Keino changed to the steeplechase and won a second Olympic victory at Munich in 1972.

Koch, Marita (East Germany), sprinter, born 1957. She was the outstanding women's winner in the 1978 European Championships in Prague, with a world-record time for the 400 metres of 48·94 sec.; she was also the star of the European Cup final in Turin in 1979 with yet another world record of 48·6 sec. and set a world 200 metres record of 21·71 sec.

Konihowski, Diane (Canada), pentathlete, born 1951. Formerly Diane Jones. She won the 1978 Commonwealth Games pentathlon with a record score of 4,768 points for the five events, including a high jump of 1·88 m.

Kuts, Vladimir (Soviet Union), distance runner, born 1927. A former boxer and skier, Kuts took up athletics at the age of twenty-two; in 1954 he became European 5,000 metres champion in the world-record time of 13 min. 56·6 sec. Several weeks later in London his front running was defeated by a dramatic late sprint by Britain's Chris Chataway, who lowered the record to 13 min. 51·6 sec. But from then on, Kuts dominated this event and the 10,000 metres, winning both gold medals at the 1956 Olympics in Melbourne. His finest 5,000 metres record of 13 min. 35 sec. lasted for eight years.

Lannaman, Sonia (Britain), sprinter, born 1956. Following the retirement of Andrea Lynch, she at last gained the title she so well deserved when she won the Commonwealth Games 100 metres. She was an indoor international when she was only fourteen, but has been sadly handicapped by muscle injuries during her career.

Makeyeva, Marina (Soviet Union), 400 metres hurdler, born 1952. After some years trying both the flat 400 metres and the pentathlon, she finally broke through with a world record of 54·78 sec. during the 1979 Spartakiad Games in Moscow. Only a few days later she won the European Cup final in 54·82 sec.

Moses, Edwin (United States), 400 metres hurdler, born 1955. The first Olympic champion in this event to use only thirteen strides between the ten hurdles, he won the gold medal at Montreal in the world-record time of 47·64 sec., winning by more than a second, the widest margin in Olympic history. In 1977 Moses, who has also run the 110 metres high hurdles in 13·5 sec. and a 400 metres relay stage in 44 sec., lowered his own world record to 47·45 sec.

Moseyev, Leonid (Soviet Union), marathon runner, born 1952. Seventh in the Montreal Olympics, Moseyev won the European title in Prague in 1978 in 2 hr 11 min. 57·5 sec. and the next summer won the Spartakiad Games marathon in Moscow after a fierce final struggle with five runners in the stadium for the last lap at the same time.

Nehemiah, Renaldo (United States), high hurdler, born 1959. An outstanding sprinter as a teenager with 10·43 sec. for 100 metres and possessing great strength, Nehemiah lowered the world record for 110 metres hurdles to 13 sec. in 1978 and has proved to be an outstanding competitor as well as a record-breaker.

Nemeth, Miklos (Hungary), javelin thrower, born 1946. Son of the 1948 Olympic hammer champion, Miklos Nemeth suffered so often from injury that he frequently disappointed his supporters in major competitions. But in the Montreal Olympics of 1976 he won the competition with an opening world record throw of 94·58 m.

Nurmi, Paavo (Finland), middle- and long-distance runner, born 1897. The greatest of all runners before the Second World War, Nurmi won nine individual or team Olympic gold medals in the Games of 1920, 1924 and 1928, and set many new world records. His first world record, for 6 miles, came in 1921, and his last, over 2 miles, ten years later. Known as the 'Flying Finn', Nurmi once recalled 'In those days there was no special training, no warming-up, no track shoes or other athletic training. But I had to work at a jog from my thirteenth year for I was an errand boy and had to deliver goods by pushcart up the steeply rising street to the railway station.' A few weeks before the 1924 Olympics in Paris, Nurmi set world records for both the 1,500 and 5,000 metres within an hour. He was to win both Olympic titles for these distances, also within an hour. Not surprisingly in 1952, when the Olympics came to the Finnish capital, Helsinki, it was Nurmi who carried the Olympic torch round the final lap of the track at the opening ceremony.

Oerter, Al (United States), discus thrower, born 1936. He was only twenty when he won his first Olympic gold medal at Melbourne in 1956 and he won the event three more times – a feat which has never been equalled by any Olympic athlete in any event. Oerter, known as the 'Man with the

Golden Arm', several times beat the world record and was always the man for the big occasion. In 1977 he returned to competition, and threw the discus more than 62 m. Oerter should always be remembered, not only for his four gold medals but also for his refusal, unlike so many other top-class throwers, ever to take illegal body-building drugs. 'Wanting to achieve,' he once told me, 'is the secret of success, not drugs.'

Ovett, Steve (Britain), middle-distance runner, born 1955. A former European junior 800 metres champion, Steve Ovett had his greatest season in 1977 when he won both the European and World Cup 1,500 metres, thanks to an explosive final spurt. Ovett, who held the British records for both 1,500 metres and the mile until the advent of Sebastian Coe, possesses so much strength that he has also been an English junior cross-country champion, won a half marathon and covered 5,000 metres in 13 min. 25 sec. Ovett was European 1,500 metres champion in 1978 and the next year was Coe's nearest rival.

Owens, Jesse (United States), sprinter and long jumper, born 1913. Middle-aged followers of athletics still swear that Jesse Owens was the greatest athlete of all time. Within seventy minutes, on 25 May 1935 at Ann Arbor, Michigan, Owens equalled or beat six world records including a long jump of 8·13 m, which was to last until 1960. At the 1936 Olympics in Berlin, Owens won the 100 and 200 metres and the long jump, taking a fourth gold medal as a member of the American 4×100 metres relay team. He has rightly been called 'the supreme physical genius of his generation', for there is evidence that he could have become, had he not turned professional at only twenty-three, the world's fastest 400 metres runner. (He also cleared 2 m in the high jump without any special training.)

Packer, Ann (Britain), middle-distance runner, born in 1942. Perhaps the most under-publicized of all this country's greatest modern athletes, Ann was an English Schools sprint champion and pentathlete who turned to the 400 metres in 1963. A year later, at the Tokyo Olympics, she finished second to the Australian Betty Cuthbert in her new favourite event and then surprised everyone, including herself, by winning a gold medal over 800 metres in the world-record time of 2 min. 1·1 sec. Before Tokyo she had only run five previous 800 metres races.

Pascoe, Alan (Britain), 400 metres hurdler, born 1947. So versatile that he also won two AAA titles as a 200 metres runner, Pascoe was at first a high hurdler, winning the European indoor title in 1969, and also gained Olympic silver and European gold medals in the 4×400 metres relay. Turning to the 400 metres hurdles he won the 1974 Commonwealth and European titles and two European Cup finals. His best time was 48·59 sec.

Peters, Mary (Britain), pentathlete, born 1939. It took seventeen years of competition in the pentathlon, training under difficult conditions in strife-torn Belfast, before Mary Peters became Olympic champion and world-record-holder at Munich in 1972. She was fourth in the 1964 Olympic pentathlon, and only ninth, handicapped by an ankle injury, in 1968, but was Commonwealth champion both in 1970 and 1974. A former British-record-holder in the shot, she achieved a personal best high jump of 1·82 m during the Munich pentathlon.

Pirie, Gordon (Britain), distance runner, born 1931. Pirie was the pioneer of modern British distance running, though he never won either an Olympic or European title. His outstanding performances included world records for 3,000 metres (7 min. 52·8 sec.) and 5,000 metres (13 min. 36·8 sec.) against the toughest opposition. He was three times English cross-country champion.

Quarrie, Donald (Jamaica), sprinter, born 1951. The greatest ever sprinter of the Commonwealth, Quarrie was first in the 1976 Montreal Olympic 200 metres and second in the 100 metres. He was three times Commonwealth Games 100 metres champion and has won a record total of six gold medals in those Games. Quarrie's fastest 200 metres is 19·86 sec.

Rand, Mary (Britain), long jumper, born 1940. Now married to the former Olympic decathlon champion, American Bill Toomey, Mary set her first British record, in the pentathlon, when she was only seventeen. As a specialist long jumper she finished only ninth in the 1960 Olympic final largely because of nerves. Four years later, in Tokyo, she won the gold medal with a world record jump of 6·76 m and also gained silver (pentathlon) and bronze (4 × 100 metres relay) medals in the same Games. A naturally talented athlete, she was a great competitor who always enjoyed her sport.

Riehm, Karl-Hans (West Germany), hammer thrower, born 1951. In 1975 he raised the world record in five instalments from 76·66 m to 78·50 m. Then, in 1978, he improved it once again to 80·32 m. Fourth in the 1976 Montreal Olympics and third in the 1978 European Championships, Riehm at last proved he could be a 'big time' competitor by winning the European Cup final in 1979.

Rono, Henry (Kenya), distance runner, born 1952. In the space of only four months in the summer of 1978 Rono set astonishing world records for 3,000 metres (7 min. 32·1 sec.), 5,000 metres (13 min. 8·4 sec.), 10,000 metres (27 min. 22·4 sec.) and 3,000 metres steeplechase (8 min. 5·4 sec.). In spite of racing here, there and everywhere, Rono still won both the 5,000 metres and the steeplechase in the 1978 Edmonton Commonwealth Games. In his world 10,000 metres record run, Rono's 5,000 metres half-way time of 13 min. 49 sec. would have been a world record up to 1955. The long-striding Kenyan, who specialized in a withering mid-race burst of speed, was not at his best during 1979.

Rudolph, Wilma (United States), sprinter, born 1940. Between the ages of four and seven Wilma Rudolph had a paralysed left leg. At sixteen, she won a bronze medal in the 1956 Olympic 4 × 100 metres relay. Four years later in Rome, this most graceful of sprinters was the winner of three gold medals in the 100 and 200 metres and the sprint relay.

Ryun, Jim (United States), middle-distance runner, born 1947. At only eighteen Ryun ran the mile in 3 min. 55·3 sec. Unlike many precocious athletes he kept improving and set world records for 880 yards (1 min. 44·9 sec.), 1,500 metres (3 min. 33·1 sec.) and the mile (3 min. 51·1 sec.). It should be remembered that Ryun, who once won an international 1,500 metres with a last lap of 49·8 sec., did not have the advantage of modern all-weather tracks. He was never an Olympic champion because he was handicapped by ill health and the high altitude of Mexico City, but he was one of the greatest of milers.

Sanderson, Tessa (Britain), javelin thrower, born 1956. A fine all-round athlete with good performances in both the 100 and 400 metres hurdles and high jump; she won the Commonwealth Games javelin in 1978 and was second in the European championships the same year. Set a United

Kingdom record of 67·20 m. in 1977 and has since been the outstanding woman field events specialist from this country.

Saneyev, Viktor (Soviet Union), triple jumper, born 1945. Saneyev switched from high jumping when he was a junior, because of a persistent knee injury; he was capable of running 100 metres in 10·5 sec. when younger. Olympic champion at Mexico City (1968), Munich (1972) and Montreal (1976); the odds must be very much against him winning a fourth title in Moscow, but he could well be in the Olympic final once again.

Schmid, Harald (West Germany), 400 metres hurdler, born 1957. The European champion of 1978. His greatest day of competition came in the 1979 European Cup final when he won both the 400 metres hurdles in a European record time of 47·85 sec. and the 400 metres in 45·31 sec. within just one hour. Schmid is capable of well under 1 min. 45 sec. for 800 metres.

Schmidt, Wolfgang (East Germany), discus thrower, born 1954. Trained by his father Ernst, a former national decathlon champion, Schmidt won the 1978 World Cup and the 1979 European Cup and has set a world discus record of 71·16 m.

Shrubb, Alfred (Britain), distance runner, born 1878. The first great British and European runner of the twentieth century, Shrubb set several records between the 1½ miles and the hour which were to last for more than thirty years. His finest season was that of 1904 but he was deprived of a chance to try for an Olympic medal in that year because Britain did not send a team to the Games in St Louis. In 1905 he became a professional athlete but he was reinstated as an amateur by the Amateur Athletic Association at the age of seventy-five.

Simeoni, Sara (Italy), high jumper, born 1953. Twice European indoor champion, Sara rose to the occasion during the 1978 European Championships in Prague when she won the high jump title and equalled her own world record of 2·01 m. On home ground, in the 1979 Turin European Cup final, she finished second to East Germany's Rosi Ackermann.

Smith, Tommie (United States), sprinter, born 1944. The greatest 200 metres runner yet seen, Tommie (Jet) Smith won the 1968 Olympic title by two metres in 19·8 sec. even though he suffered a thigh injury 20 m before the finish. His other best performances included 10·2 sec. for 100 metres, 19·5 sec. for 220 yards straight, 44·5 sec. for 400 metres (a flying 400 metres relay leg in 43·8 sec.) and a long jump of 7·90 m. On the Olympic victory rostrum Smith and his team-mate John Carlos raised black-gloved fists in a gesture of protest against the United States government's policy towards blacks and for this they were banned from the United States Olympic team.

Snell, Peter (New Zealand), middle-distance runner, born 1938. The Olympic 800 metres champion at Rome in 1960, this powerfully built athlete reached the climax of his competitive career when he won both the 800 and 1,500 metres Olympic titles at Tokyo four years later. This was the first time since 1920 that such a double had been achieved (by Britain's Albert Hill). Snell's world records included 880 yards, on a grass-track, in 1 min. 44·3 sec. and a mile in 3 min. 54·1 sec.

Stewart, Ian (Britain), distance runner, born 1949. Brother of internationals Mary and Peter, Ian Stewart was the European 5,000 metres champion in 1969 and the Commonwealth winner the following year. In 1975 he won the European indoor 3,000 metres in Poland and, just one week later, the international cross-country title over $7\frac{1}{2}$ miles in the heat of north Africa.

Szewińska, Irena (Poland), sprinter, born 1946. At the Tokyo Olympics of 1964, when she was only eighteen, Irena Kirszenstein, as she then was, won silver medals in the long jump and 200 metres, and a gold in the 4×100 metres relay. In 1968 she was Olympic 200 metres champion and third in the 100 metres. In 1972 she finished third in the Olympic 200 metres and the next season became the first woman to beat 50 sec. for the 400 metres. It was over this distance that she won the Montreal Olympic gold medal in a then world-record time of 49·29 sec. Her friendly personality and complete lack of conceit has earned her the title of 'Queen of the Track'.

Thompson, Daley (Britain), decathlete, born 1958. In 1976 Daley competed in the Montreal Olympic decathlon, an invaluable experience for a youngster. In 1977 he won the European junior title and the next summer he won the Edmonton Commonwealth Games gold medal just one week after his twentieth birthday with a points score of 8,467, the third highest of all time. This tall Londoner came excitingly close to beating the world decathlon record in 1979 but failed at his opening height in the pole vault because his own three personal poles had been lost. Thompson, the most promising all-rounder in the history of athletics, may be capable of 10·3 sec. for 100 metres, 47 sec. for 400 metres, 8·15 m in the long jump and 5 m for the pole vault, *during a decathlon*.

Thompson, Ian (Britain), marathon runner, born 1949. After winning the 1973 AAA marathon title in 2 hr 12 min. 40 sec., the fastest ever début over the distance, Thompson went on to become the Commonwealth Games and Euro-

pean champion in 1974. His best time was for the Commonwealth gold medal in New Zealand with 2 hr 9 min. 12 sec. –
at that time the fastest ever in a major championship.

Thorpe, Jim (United States), decathlete, born 1888. The first
great all-rounder of modern athletics, Thorpe won both the
pentathlon and the decathlon in the 1912 Olympics but was
subsequently disqualified for life because it was discovered
he had been paid small sums for playing baseball in 1909
and 1910.

Tkachenko, Nadyezhda (Soviet Union), pentathlete, born
1948. The world-record-holder, with 4,839 points in the new
version of the pentathlon which includes an 800 metres as
the fifth and final event. She won the European title in
Prague in 1978 but was subsequently disqualified from that
competition for taking the illegal anabolic steroids. She was
reinstated in time for the 1980 Olympics in Moscow.

Tyus, Wyomia (United States), sprinter, born 1945. The first
sprinter, male or female, to retain an Olympic title, she won
her first Olympic 100 metres at Tokyo in 1964 and her
second in Mexico City in 1968.

Viren, Lasse (Finland), distance runner, born 1949. The
outstanding distance competitor of modern athletics; he
won both the 5,000 and 10,000 metres in successive Olympics. In Munich in 1972 Viren's winning times were 13 min.
26·4 sec. and 27 min. 38·4 sec. (a world record even though
Viren fell just before half-way) and in Montreal in 1976 his
times were 13 min. 24·8 sec. and 27 min. 40·4 sec. Viren,
who brought to an almost magical art the capacity to be at
his best on the most important days of competition, took
part in his first marathon in Montreal, just one day after the
5,000 metres final, and finished fifth.

Walker, John (New Zealand), middle-distance runner, born 1952. He first made his mark in the 1974 Commonwealth Games when he finished second to the world-record-breaking Filbert Bayi of Tanzania. In 1975 Walker became the first man to beat 3 min. 50 sec. for the mile with his time of 3 min. 49·4 sec. – exactly 10 sec. faster than the first breaching of the four-minute barrier by Britain's Roger Bannister twenty-one years earlier. He was the Olympic 1,500 metres champion of 1976 and returned to competition in 1979 after many months' inactivity through injury.

Wells, Allan (Britain), sprinter, born 1952. Wells broke into world class in 1978 when his victory in Edmonton in the 200 metres meant that he was the first United Kingdom athlete to win a Commonwealth sprint title for forty years. Holder of the British 100 metres record at 10·15 sec. from 1978, he set a 200 metres record of 20·56 sec. the following season and then became the first European for six years to beat, over 200 metres, the Italian Pietro Mennea in the European Cup final.

Wooderson, Sydney (Britain), middle-distance runner, born 1914. No British runner has ever had such a remarkably long career at the top. In 1937 the slightly built Wooderson set a world mile record of 4 min. 6·4 sec. The next year he lowered the records for both 800 metres (1 min. 48·4 sec.) and 880 yards (1 min. 49·2 sec.) before winning the European 1,500 metres title. After five years of war service, Wooderson returned to athletics to win the 1946 European 5,000 metres title with a powerful last lap sprint, having improved his best mile to 4 min. 4·2 sec. the previous season. In 1948 he bowed out triumphantly by winning the English cross-country title over 9 miles at the age of thirty-three.

Yashchenko, Vladimir (Soviet Union), high jumper, born 1959. He lifted the world record to 2·33 m in 1977, when he was also European junior champion, using the straddle technique rather than the Fosbury flop. Just 1·94 tall, he increased the world record to 2·34 m in 1978, when he also won the European title. Indoors he has cleared 2·35 m, but indoor performances cannot be considered as official world records.

Zatopek, Emil (Czechoslovakia), distance runner, born 1922. Olympic 10,000 metres champion in London in 1948 and then 5,000, 10,000 and marathon winner at Helsinki in 1952, Zatopek was regarded as the outstanding competitor in distance running until the advent of Lasse Viren of Finland. The first man to beat 29 min. for 10,000 metres, he was far in advance of his own generation through his vigorous training methods. Through the warmth of his personality and his gift for languages he has remained a hero to the scores of athletes, all over the world, who have beaten his best performances of 13 min. 57 sec. (5,000 metres), 28 min. 54·2 sec. (10,000 metres) and 20,052 m in one hour. If I had to choose my favourite athlete of all my years in the sport then the choice would almost certainly be Emil Zatopek.

5 A Guide to the Athletics Programme

The sprints (100, 200 and 400 metres)

Sprinting is the most developed of all the track and field skills. In the average minor sports meeting the biggest entry will always be for the sprint race. Men and women's records for the 100 metres are nowadays shaved by one hundredths of a second, rather than 'shattered', because in such a short, popular event there is little room for improvement compared with, say, the pole vault or the 1,500 metres.

In sprinting over 100 metres the coach looks for an explosive start, great acceleration from the start to around 30 m (known as the pick-up stage), a sustained speed from about 40 m to 60 m and then a slight deceleration, or slowing down, for the remainder of the race.

The sprinter needs the physical strength to drive powerfully away from the starting blocks which, incidentally, are not compulsory but were introduced during the 1930s when sprinters had to dig starting holes in the loose cinder track. They should also strive for maximum stride length and leg speed. In top-class sprinting the athletes are moving at a rate of about six strides per second.

At the start, the feet must be in contact with the ground, not only with the blocks. Fingers must be behind the line and the starter must make sure that all athletes are steady on their marks when he gives the command 'set'. The normal interval between 'set' and the firing of the gun is between 1·5 sec. and 3·0 sec. Any athlete in any event having two false starts is disqualified from the race.

The finishing line, rather than the tape (which is only used as a visual guide by the judges), is the official finish. Most top-class meetings will have a photo-finish. An electrical timing device is usually installed for accuracy of judging and timing.

The 200 metres is run on a curve in lanes with a staggered start, with the blocks set on the outside of the bend. This means that the runner can move in a straight line for the opening strides in order to achieve better rhythm and relaxation. The 200 metres runner has to be able to maintain relaxation and, almost imperceptibly, to coast during a brief part of the curve. The runner must learn to run the bend with just the right body angle to maintain speed.

The 400 metres, one full circuit of the track run in lanes, obviously needs more strength than the shorter sprints. That strength has to be acquired in training with, for example, repetition runs over 200 or 300 metres. Pace judgement is essential, too, so that running effort is distributed economically. An international athlete aiming for, say, 46·4 sec., would probably try for 22·2 sec. for the first half of the race and 24·2 sec. for the second half. Energy, and style, must be reserved for the second stage. The world's greatest 400 metres specialists today are capable of averaging close to 11 sec. for the four successive 100 m. Even a first-class senior schoolboy athlete might aim at averaging 12·5 sec., for a total time of 50 sec., and a first-class senior girl might aim at 13·5 sec., for a total of 54 sec.

The relays (4 × 100 metres and 4 × 400 metres)

Winning a sprint relay is not just a question of putting together four top-class sprinters. They must learn correct technique, for it is the relay baton, a smooth hollow tube measuring between 0·28 m and 0·30 m, and weighing not less than 50 g, which has to be kept moving at speed over the whole distance.

Relay runners must exchange the baton within the limits of a 20 m zone. The outgoing runner has another 10 m behind the zone, or 'box', in which to accelerate before taking the baton. Only constant practice between members of the team, using check marks on the track, can avoid a fatal slowing up of the baton at the time of the exchange.

Any changes made outside the box call for disqualification and if the baton is actually dropped, as has happened even in the Olympic Games, it must be picked up by the runner who dropped it.

The baton is usually passed with a sweeping, upward motion into the receiving runner's open hand. In the 4×100 metres relay the runners do not look back once they have seen the incoming sprinter reach the agreed check mark. In the 4×400 metres relay, however, the incoming runner is often tiring and, after the first one and a half 'legs', the race is not run in lanes. So the waiting runner must keep a close eye on his team-mate, often waving at him to catch his attention as he approaches the exchange area.

Middle distances (800 and 1,500 metres)

You may hear coaches refer to these events as aerobic (with oxygen) distances. By this they mean that for the middle distances there is time – indeed it is necessary – to use the heart and circulation system to provide continuing energy, whereas in the anaerobic (without oxygen) sprints the runner is mainly using muscle.

This is not as complicated as it sounds at first. To take an example, it is considered that the 800 metres requires 33 per cent aerobic and 67 per cent anaerobic effort. As you move up distance to the 1,500 metres the distribution becomes

50–50, because now there is an equal need for strength and speed.

For the middle-distance athlete in training there must be the right mixture of long slowish running – say a five-mile run on the road or grass at a pace of 6 min. per mile – and interval training on the track with perhaps 10×200 metres at 80 per cent effort with breaks of barely a minute. With this kind of training diet, though at a far more strenuous level, great middle-distance runners like Britain's Sebastian Coe and Steve Ovett sharpen and toughen themselves.

Since the 800 metres is run in lane only for the first turn, and the 1,500 metres is not run in lanes at all, racing tactics and strategy, knowing when to lead and when to follow, avoiding being boxed-in by the field, are very important. Even the strongest middle-distance runners hesitate to lead from gun to tape, especially if it is a windy afternoon and the opposition is of international class. Many great modern racers prefer to launch their final attack from the middle of the last back straight though much will depend upon the speed of the opening lap in the 800 metres or the first three laps over 1,500 metres.

Middle-distance runners, like sprinters, use light weight-lifting to build up strength in their winter training and practise stretching exercises daily during their warm-up to ensure that their limbs and tendons are supple. All middle-distance runners have to possess fine pace judgement so that, ideally, they can distribute their effort evenly over the whole distance and get the very best out of themselves in competition.

Long distance (5,000 and 10,000 metres for men, 3,000 metres for women)

The modern distance runner does an extraordinary amount of running in training to build up endurance. It is not advisable for athletes of under seventeen to do too much but seniors at the highest level may cover 100 miles a week, especially during the winter.

Runners undertaking this kind of mileage need to take scrupulous care of their feet and legs and avoid stress injuries. In their training they include daily stretching of feet and legs. It is important, too, to have well padded running shoes. Care of the feet is just as important for the thousands who, both in Britain and in the United States, now practise 'jogging', very slow long-distance running, for basic fitness.

In long-distance running there is obviously a much greater chance than in the middle distances of being able to run right away from the opposition because the athlete has more time to make strength tell. A champion like Britain's Brendan Foster has been known to make a winning break with at least three laps to go in a 5,000 metres or with seven to go over 10,000 metres, but he had to be very confident in his own ability to succeed with that kind of breakaway tactic.

The marathon

The marathon represents a huge step forward from the 10,000 metres since it measures 26 miles 385 yards, or 42,195 m, on the road. Yet there are now thousands of men, women and youngsters running the marathon in the United States, hoping simply for a feeling of pride at having finished, rather than a fast time.

The world's top men marathon runners are capable of a

pace close to 5 min. per mile for the whole distance. The women's best performance (there are no official world marathon records since the event is run on the road rather than an exactly measured track) could soon be under 2 hr 25 min. and the target for men may soon be 2 hr 5 min.

The marathon runner sometimes trains for up to 125 miles a week including perhaps an 18–20-mile run at the weekend. But he or she is unlikely to have more than three serious marathon races in a year, so severe is the effect upon the body.

During a marathon race soft drinks are provided at approximately every 5,000 metres, as well as sponging stations, which are very necessary in warm weather. A marathon runner can sometimes lose several pounds in body weight during a race. No one should ever consider taking part even in a half-marathon without proper training and expert advice.

Hurdling (110 metres and 400 metres for men, 100 metres and 400 metres for women, 3,000 metres steeplechase for men)

Basically hurdling is about sprinting, spring and suppleness. Flexibility, because of the unnatural position demanded of the body when hurdling the fences, is absolutely vital and both hurdlers and steeplechasers should exercise every day of their athletic career.

The right stride pattern is essential or else one will be in danger of the hurdle ending round one's neck. For the short-distance hurdles, most athletes take eight strides to the first obstacle, though for the long-legged it might be seven strides or nine for the short-legged. The hurdles are then three strides apart. (The hurdles are 1·067 m high for men, 0·84 m high for women).

The athlete aims to attack the hurdle with a fiercely thrust out leading leg with the following leg parallel to the top of the hurdle. Ideally, the athlete just clears the top of the barrier (to go too high would be time-wasting) and then lands with shoulders and hips already moving forward for the next stride and the next hurdle. This may sound far more simple than it proves to be. Sprint hurdlers need to practise constantly until the right stride pattern is engraved upon the subconscious.

The 400 metres hurdler must have stamina as well as speed and suppleness, should be capable of a fast time over the flat training distances of 500 and 600 metres. Obviously they need to be tall although not as tall as for the sprint hurdles. (The hurdles in the 400 metres men's hurdles are 0·914 m high.)

In the 400 metres there is 35 m spacing between each pair of hurdles and this allows for different kinds of stride patterns. Some athletes strive for fifteen strides between the ten hurdles all the way; some take fifteen until they get tired and then deliberately switch to seventeen; those who have trained to hurdle off either foot, might try fourteen strides and fifteen in the later stages. Edwin Moses, who won the 1976 Olympic title for the United States, was the first gold medal winner to use thirteen strides all the way.

During training the 400 metres hurdler has to re-create competitive situations by hurdling in different stages of fatigue so that there will be no need, in a race, to chop the stride through a mixture of exhaustion and panic.

All hurdlers are trying to make their times as near as possible to their speed on the flat, when there are none of the annoying fences in the way. A woman 100 metres hurdler should try to come within 1·5–2 sec. of her flat 100 metres time; a male hurdler over 110 metres aims to come within 3–4 sec. of his 100 metres flat time. In the 400 metres hurdles the differential should be between 2·5 sec. and 3·5 sec. All hurdlers must be confident, refusing to be inhibited by the obstacle in front of them, remembering the old saying 'Treat every hurdle as if it was the winning post.'

The 3,000 metres steeplechase combines middle-distance strength and tactics plus hurdling's judgement and suppleness. The name comes from nineteenth-century races on horseback between the steeples of various churches. The modern steeplechaser has to clear seven water jumps and twenty-eight hurdles spread over the 3,000 metres. The water jump is 366 cm wide and 70 cm deep and the barrier in front of the water jump is 91·4 cm high, as is each hurdle.

A first-class steeplechaser like Britain's Denis Coates hopes to take about 1 sec. to clear each water jump, without suffering any real interruption to the rhythm of his running. None the less, the steeplechaser has to face thirty-five possible interruptions to his concentration; he may also find himself crowded by other runners as he comes up to the hurdle because there are no lanes in this event.

The steeplechaser must therefore practise many times by pushing with one foot off the hurdle in front of the water jump and then landing in the shallows about 30 cm from the edge of the water. Both legs must be able to lead.

Ideally the runner aims at covering the steeplechase in only 35 sec. less than his best time for 3,000 metres on the flat. Much easier said than done. All hurdlers must learn to combine their headlong rush with polished technique.

Walking (20,000 and 50,000 metres for men)

The essential difference, as far as the rules of athletics are concerned, between running and walking is that in race-walking the strides must be made so that one foot is in contact with the ground all the time. A walker who fails to do that, and is adjudged to be 'lifting', gets only one warning. For a second offence he is disqualified.

Race-walkers have a special technique to learn. What they are aiming at is totally different from going for a casual stroll round town. Correct walking action, with its rolling of hips and bottom, may seem funny to the ignorant spectator. But the athletic walker deserves warm applause rather than laughter. The sport demands flexibility, endurance and complete concentration, and its participants are noted for their friendliness.

The Jumps

Long jump

This is the simplest of the four jumping events in that natural speed and spring can produce a good leap without much detailed technical training. But the long jump is not, as has been claimed light-heartedly, 'just running for a while and then taking off'. The world's best specialists, capable of over 8 m in the men's event and more than 6·50 m in the women's, have to work for many hours in training.

Long jumpers must follow a fast run-up with a change of rhythm in the last three strides in order to achieve a powerful take-off from the board placed at the end of the runway and not less than 1 m from the landing area. Top men jumpers generally have an approach run of 40–45 m and women 30–35 metres.

In mid-air there are different styles for trying to maintain the body in a good position for landing, including the hitch-kick and the hang. The actual jump, provided the athlete has not 'fouled' by taking off after the board, is measured from the nearest point at which she or he has landed.

The current world record which is expected to last longest is that of 8·90 m for the long jump by the American Bob

Beamon in the 1968 Olympics, when he was aided both by the maximum possible wind, for record ratification, of 2 metres per second and the 'thin' atmosphere of high-altitude Mexico City. Even Beamon himself once told me, three years after his feat, 'I still can't quite believe I jumped that far.' But he did.

Pole vault

The introduction of fibre-glass poles in the late 1950s, replacing metal poles, revolutionized this demanding, spectacular event which is practised only by men. The elasticity of the new poles, now used by all vaulters, allowed the athlete a higher hand hold and that meant that records began to fall at a fast rate.

Pole vaulting calls for outstanding gymnastic ability, strength and courage. Great patience, too, for the pattern of movement which has to be learned is complicated. The vaulter must possess both sprinting speed and the force to give the pole the maximum useful bend for a high hand grip. His back and arms must be strong and he must have a quick mind to cope with the various body position changes as he sails up towards a bar balanced at 5–5·5 m, after planting his pole in the sloping take-off box sunk level in the ground in front of the uprights.

After the vaulter has cleared the bar in a fly-away, arching movement he has to make sure that the pole is released so that it does not dislodge the bar. Three consecutive failures rule him out of the competition. On the happily rare occasions when a pole breaks in mid-air it does not count as a failure – though the vaulter may sometimes be too shaken to continue.

High jump

The two main styles in international competition are the straddle, in which the athlete crosses the bar, stomach downwards – he appears to be draped round the bar – and the Fosbury flop, in which the jumper, having used a curving approach run, achieves a back bend that whips his trunk over the bar before his legs.

The flop was made famous by the 1968 Olympic victory of the American Dick Fosbury though there had been other experimental versions in the earlier years of the sport. For beginners it must be emphasized that it is dangerous to try the 'flop' unless a well-padded, built-up landing area is available.

All high jumpers should aim for a balanced approach run, gathering their bodies for an explosion upwards after a long last stride. In the past too many British jumpers thought more about a perfect clearance of the bar rather than an aggressive take-off in order to gain height.

The high jumper must take off from one foot. Three consecutive failures disqualify the athlete from further jumping. As in the pole vault, international competitions can take many hours to complete, so the high jumper needs both endurance and considerable powers of concentration.

Triple jump

Sometimes still called the hop, step and jump, the international label (*dreisprung* in German, *triple saut* in French) is more suitable because there are three separate jumps even though they have to be smoothly linked together and one effort should not offset a later one.

Triple jumpers tend not to be as fast as long jumpers but they have to possess great leg power. According to international rules the hop and the step must be made with the same leg and the final jump with the other leg. How the athlete tries to break up the jumps in distance depends upon whether his coach, or his basic athletic ability, turns him to the Polish technique or the Russian style.

An example of the Polish flat style could be a ratio of 35 per cent hop, 30 per cent step and 35 per cent jump. This is likely to be favoured by the sprinter-triple jumper whereas the strong-legged, bounding type of jumper might prefer the Russian division of 38 per cent, 30 per cent, 32 per cent. What all triple jumpers must aim for is a high horizontal speed and a rhythm which can sound, as they strike the ground, almost like a drum-beat.

The Throws

Shot put

The simplest of the four throwing events in technique, it began in various Celtic sports meetings as 'putting the stone'. Putting is not throwing as the rules make clear by stating that the athlete cannot take the shot away from his neck before he pushes rather than throws it.

The shot used by men weighs 7·26 kg and is put from a circle with a maximum diameter of 2·135 m. For women the shot weighs 4 kg. A foul throw is registered if the athlete puts a foot on the top of the stop-board fixed to the front of the circle or does not walk out of the back of the circle after the put.

The athlete begins by facing the back of the circle. Then he or she drives the body off the right leg, low and fast across the circle, before rotating hips and chest square on to the front of the circle so that the putting arm can complete the movement and release the shot.

Italy's Dorando Pietri, accompanied by his refreshment official, wearily wends his way towards the White City stadium where he is to be disqualified from winning the 1908 Olympic marathon (*All-Sport*)

Paavo Nurmi, the Flying Finn, as most spectators in the 1920s saw him, alone, poised, far ahead of his rivals in middle and distance running (*L'Equipe*)

Jesse Owens, the greatest athlete of the 1930s, sails out for yet another victory in the long jump, the event in which this great sprinter set a world record lasting for twenty-five years (*L'Equipe*)

Bursting away at the start of what is to be history's first sub-four-minute mile, Chris Brasher leads Roger Bannister, the winner, and Chris Chataway on the evening of 6 May 1954 at Iffley Road, Oxford (*Ed Lacey*)

British Olympic gold at its greatest. Four 1964 champions: from left to right, Ken Matthews (walk), Ann Packer (800 metres), Mary Rand (long jump) and Lynn Davies (long jump) (*Ed Lacey*)

Top left: Dick Fosbury, the 1968 Olympic high jump winner whose surname, used to describe his back clearance of the bar, has immortalized him in the technical history of the sport (*All-Sport*)

Below left: A multiple world-record-breaker in full cry. Henry Rono of Kenya, the distance-running marvel of 1978, begins to apply pressure from the front (*All-Sport*)

Below: No one ever believed that Miklos Nemeth of Hungary was a big-time competitor until he won the 1976 Olympic javelin title with a world-record throw (*Ed Lacey*)

Arms spread wide, Britain's Brendan Foster wins a European Cup 5,000 metres final with a grin for his fans (*Ed Lacey*)

Britain's Mary Peters, strain clearly marked on her face, drives through the 200 metres, then the final event of the pentathlon, to win the Olympic title at Munich in 1972 (*Ed Lacey*)

Top left: Al Oerter of the United States, the only athlete in the modern Olympics to win four successive gold medals, builds up for his explosive discus release within the throwers' protective cage (*Ed Lacey*)

Below left: American super sprinter Tommie Smith (right) heads Lee Evans over 440 yards (*Track and Field News*)

Below: Strength and speed. Lasse Viren of Finland leads East Germany's Manfred Kuschmann and Britain's Tony Simmons over 10,000 metres (*Ed Lacey*)

Every hurdle must be treated as a winning post. Britain's Alan Pascoe (left) winning the 1974 European 400 metres hurdles title from Jean-Claude Nallet of France (*Ed Lacey*)

Tatyana Kazankina of the Soviet Union won both the 800 and 1,500 metres in the 1976 Olympics. Here she gains invaluable strength by finishing second in the international cross-country championships the same year (*Ed Lacey*)

Daley Thompson throwing the javelin in the decathlon at the
Commonwealth Games in 1978 (*All-Sport*)

With a twinkle in his eye, Britain's Steve Ovett, the European 1,500 metres champion, breaks the tape looking completely relaxed (*Ed Lacey*)

A world record to last to the twenty-first century? American Bob Beamon long jumps an incredible 8.90m in the 1968 Olympics (*Ed Lacey*)

All throwers need to train for technique, strength (weight-lifting at least three times a week during the winter and spring), mobility and speed. A top-class shot-putter like the British record-holder Geoff Capes is a fine short-distance sprinter for all his massive size.

Discus throw

The discus specialist is trying to follow a similar pattern to the shot-putter, using first the strongest muscles of the body and then faster arm movements. But there are major problems which the shot-putter does not face.

The discus thrower not only moves forward in the circle of 2·5 m diameter but uses a kind of running turn calling for fine balance. The difference between a standing throw and a turning throw is that the thrower is out to accelerate the discus (which weighs 2 kg for men and 1 kg for women) continuously on the longest possible path before the release.

The athlete starts by facing away from the direction of the throw, makes a couple of preliminary swings and then, taking the weight firmly on the ball of the left foot, drives forward across the circle fast and low. The thrower lands on a bent right leg and then completes the turn by planting the left leg down firmly at the front of the circle but a little to the left of the line of throwing. The right leg lifts power-fully over the firmly braced left leg, driving the hips and shoulders ahead of the discus as the throwing arm goes into a long slinging action.

Ideally the discus goes spinning away from the first finger – ideally, because the spinning release and the half flat angle of the discus in the air is vital in an event in which, unlike the shot, varying wind conditions can make a great deal of difference to the distance achieved within the official landing sector of 45° beyond the circle.

Hammer throw

The only throwing event not practised by women. Distances achieved at international level have improved vastly through the work of coaches from the Soviet Union and West and East Germany.

The hammer itself, originally a sledgehammer as used on farms in Ireland and Scotland, now consists of three parts, a metal head, a wire and a hand grip. The total weight must not be less than 7·26 kg and the throwing circle has an inside diameter of 2·135 m. For hammer throwing a protective cage is essential for this can be a dangerous event, especially now that distances of between 76 and 80 metres are being attained.

The initial velocity of the hammer naturally determines the length it flies. The thrower gives the hammer a couple of preliminary swings and then turns three times on his left foot in the circle with a push-off from the right leg at each turn. In the first section of the turn the competitor pivots on the heel and in the second part on the ball of the foot.

Each time the athlete turns he is accelerating the hammer, trying to keep the sweep of the hammer as long as possible. He tries to get his hips ahead of his shoulders and his shoulders ahead of the hammer until the moment of explosive release when, with a whip-lash effect, the long wire and hammer head goes up and away.

Javelin throw

Like the discus throw, this event can be traced back to the ancient Greek Games, whereas the shot and hammer stem from Celtic sports. Unlike the other three throws, the javelin has no definite rule laid down for the length of the run-up.

The javelin has to be thrown from behind the arc of a

circle of 8 m radius. It must be held at the specially taped grip and the thrower cannot turn and whirl but must always face the throwing direction. To register a valid throw the tip of the metal head must touch the ground first.

The minimum weight of the javelin is 800 g for men, 600 g for women; it must measure between 260 cm and 270 cm for men and between 220 cm and 230 cm for women.

Throwing the javelin a long way needs a far more exact technique than, say, throwing a cricket ball, even though both activities demand a strong shoulder and arm. Most beginners are extremely disappointed when they hurl the javelin with all their might and find it comes down, often twisting awkwardly, a very short distance away.

The approach run is vital and must carry through smoothly into the pulling back of arm and spear and then the throwing of the javelin. With a proper run-up, the well-coached junior athlete may achieve nearly 25 m further than with a standing throw.

Top-class javelin throwers tend to use either a five- or seven-stride approach. The athlete must get the stride pattern exactly right so that there is a minimum loss of speed when the long javelin is released overhand. As in all the throwing events there must be a smooth follow-through. The javelin thrower shares with the discus thrower the aerodynamic problem of 'flighting' the javelin at the right angle through the air.

All javelin throwing, especially at school or junior level, should be supervised by a teacher or coach so that there is no risk of injury or even death caused by athletes running forward to retrieve their spears when others are about to throw.

The All-Rounders

Decathlon (for men)

The basic programme of this challenging event, in which individual performances are rated on an international points scoring table, is as follows:

First day: 100 metres, long jump, shot put, high jump, 400 metres.

Second day: 110 metres hurdles, discus throw, pole vault, javelin throw, 1,500 metres.

At the end of two exhausting days, the points for each of the ten performances (e.g., 1,000 points for a 100 metres in 10·3 sec. or a javelin throw of 81 metres) are added together to find the overall winner. The decathlon demands not only extraordinary versatility but also mental adaptation and muscular coordination. The modern decathlon champion cannot afford to have any really weak event. Therefore it is not surprising that Britain's superb decathlon record-holder, Daley Thompson, is also outstanding nationally as a sprinter and long jumper.

Most important of all, the decathlete must be able to switch from one kind of athletic skill to a very different one within a matter of minutes. Consequently, *combined* training for the ten events should be followed systematically, practising the events in the order in which they will be held during a decathlon competition: training sessions of, for example, sprinting followed by long jumping or high hurdling followed by discus throwing reflect the actual decathlon programme.

Pentathlon (for women)

The official programme for this two-day event, in which individual performances are, as in the decathlon, rated on an international points scoring table, is as follows:

First day: 100 metres hurdles, shot put, high jump.

Second day: long jump, 800 metres.

When Britain's Mary Peters won the Olympic pentathlon at Munich in 1972 the final event was a 200 metres race. It was the same at the Montreal Olympics of 1976. But now the 800 metres has been included instead, in order to test endurance as well as speed.

The woman pentathlete need not be particularly tall but she must be strong enough for the shot put and she must also have good spring for she has to face two jumping events. But there may have to be some rethinking about basic pentathlon preparation now that times of under 2 min. 10 sec. for the final 800 metres are likely to be necessary if an athlete wishes to finish high in an Olympic final.

This brief examination of the wide programme of events in the international athletics programme is *not* meant to be a coaching guide. It must be underlined that the young athlete who wants to do well needs both a qualified coach and an efficient, friendly club. It must be recognized, too, that the considerable differences between the regulations (weight of throwing implements, height of hurdles, distances in running) for seniors and juniors have been drawn up to stop youngsters slavishly imitating those with older, stronger bodies.

Most important of all, the young boy or girl taking up track and field athletics should do so in a mood of exploration rather than specialization. Scores of sensible coaching books exist, many of them to be found in the local library. But the most valuable advice of all is: 'Start slowly and always try to have fun.'

6 Exercises for Athletics

By a physiotherapist

We all know that people normally take part in sport because they want to maintain their fitness and health. A short session of preliminary exercises, or warm-up, just before training and competition, helps to prepare the body for more efficient exercise and also helps to prevent injuries.

The effect of these exercises should be both physiological and psychological. One of the aims is to raise the general body temperature and the temperature of the deep muscle tissues; this automatically accelerates the rate at which the body cells work. The flow of blood to the muscles is improved and the muscles receive a better supply of oxygen. It also means that the waste products of the cells are efficiently removed.

Warm-up exercises should gently stretch the muscles and other soft tissues, thus improving their flexibility and reducing the chance of them being injured during more vigorous activity.

Another important effect of the warm-up is that the speed at which the nerve impulses travel between the muscles and brain is increased. The body is therefore further prepared to work more efficiently and the mind is ready for competition.

The warm-up should be strenuous enough to be effective and produce a light sweating but without causing tiredness. These should be the aims:

1. Gentle exercise to increase the rate at which the body works and loosens up.

2. Some gently stretching exercises to help avoid injury.

3. Some specific exercises for the particular event for which the athlete is training.

It is also important to be dressed for comfort and warmth throughout.

Loosening up

Gentle running/jogging

Start by moving at a comfortable pace, either on the spot or over a distance. Continue for a few minutes, until the body feels as if it is getting going, and stop before you get tired.

Step-ups

Find a block or step of comfortable height and make sure it is fixed so that it will not slip. Start by stepping lightly

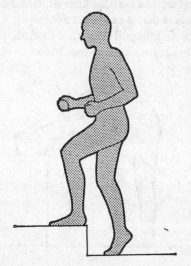

up with alternate feet on and off the block. Gradually increase your speed.

Stretching exercises

It is very important to remember that you are doing these exercises to try and avoid injury. You should hold yourself in the position where you feel the muscle start to stretch but *not* pull. A pulling feeling means that you are over-stretching the muscle and could damage it.

Hold the position of stretch for a few moments and then let go slowly.

Repeat each stretch several times – slowly and *gently*.

Hamstring stretch

Stand on one leg and keep the knee straight. Place your other leg on a support that is a comfortable height. Keep that knee straight too. Gently pull your foot towards you with your hands and lower your head to your knee.

Thigh muscle stretch

Stand on one leg and keep that knee straight. Hold the
other leg behind your back with your hands. It is important
that you do not bend at the hip or waist.

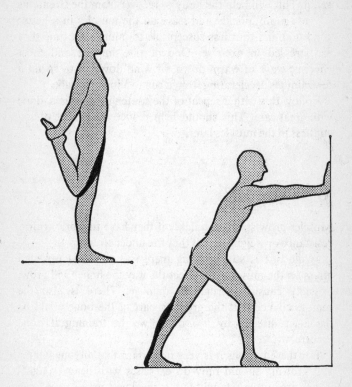

Calf muscle stretch

Stand at arm's length from a wall in a walk or stride stance.
Keep the back leg straight at the knee and the heel flat on
the floor. Take the weight over the front bent leg and push
against the wall, feeling the stretch in the back leg.

Warm down

Following a spell of intensive, vigorous exercise it is important to spend a few minutes helping the body slow down again. This will help the body to recover from the strenuous exercise more quickly and leave all the muscles in a better condition and thus less susceptible to injury next time they are stressed in exercise. One of the simplest and most effective ways of warm down, or wind down, is to spend a few minutes decelerating from a run to a jog to a walk.

Follow this with a repeat of the stretching exercises, done with great care. This should help reduce the chance of any stiffness in the muscles later.

Weight training

Muscles grow stronger quickly if they have to work against resistance or weights and if they are under stress.

While one is still growing there is a risk that repeated stress on the muscles can affect the way the bones will grow, possibly causing permanent damage. There is also the remote chance that the growing part of the bone could be damaged directly by too much weight training if done incorrectly.

For these reasons it is very important that anyone who is still growing should only do exercises with heavy weights if they are properly taught by a trained person.

7 Records and Champions

(collated by Melvyn Watman, Editor of *Athletics Weekly*)

World Records
(as ratified by the IAAF)

Men

100 metres
sec.

10·6	Donald Lippincott (USA)	6.7.1912
10·6	Jackson Scholz (USA)	16.9.1920
10·4	Charles Paddock (USA)	23.4.1921
10·4	Eddie Tolan (USA)	8.8.1929
10·4	Eddie Tolan (USA)	25.8.1929
10·3	Percy Williams (Canada)	9.8.1930
10·3	Eddie Tolan (USA)	1.8.1932
10·3	Ralph Metcalfe (USA)	12.8.1933
10·3	Eulace Peacock (USA)	6.8.1934
10·3	Christiaan Berger (Netherlands)	26.8.1934
10·3	Ralph Metcalfe (USA)	15.9.1934
10·3	Ralph Metcalfe (USA)	23.9.1934
10·3	Takayoshi Yoshioka (Japan)	15.6.1935
10·2	Jesse Owens (USA)	20.6.1936
10·2	Harold Davis (USA)	6.6.1941
10·2	Lloyd La Beach (Panama)	15.5.1948
10·2	Barney Ewell (USA)	9.7.1948
10·2	McDonald Bailey (GB)	25.8.1951
10·2	Heinz Futterer (Germany)	31.10.1954
10·2	Bobby Morrow (USA)	19.5.1956

100 metres – *contd*

sec.

10·2	Ira Murchison (USA)	1.6.1956
10·2	Bobby Morrow (USA)	22.6.1956
10·2	Ira Murchison (USA)	29.6.1956
10·2	Bobby Morrow (USA)	29.6.1956
10·1	Willie Williams (USA)	3.8.1956
10·1	Ira Murchison (USA)	4.8.1956
10·1	Leamon King (USA)	20.10.1956
10·1	Leamon King (USA)	27.10.1956
10·1	Ray Norton (USA)	18.4.1959
10·0	Armin Hary (Germany)	21.6.1960
10·0	Harry Jerome (Canada)	15.7.1960
10·0	Horacio Esteves (Venezuela)	15.8.1964
10·0	Bob Hayes (USA)	15.10.1964
10·0	Jim Hines (USA)	27.5.1967
10·0	Enrique Figuerola (Cuba)	17.6.1967
10·0	Paul Nash (S. Africa)	2.4.1968
10·0	Oliver Ford (USA)	31.5.1968
10·0	Charlie Greene (USA)	20.6.1968
10·0	Roger Bambuck (France)	20.6.1968
9·9	Jim Hines (USA)	20.6.1968
9·9	Ronnie Ray Smith (USA)	20.6.1968
9·9	Charlie Greene (USA)	20.6.1968
9·9	Jim Hines (USA)	14.10.1968
9·9	Eddie Hart (USA)	1.7.1972
9·9	Rey Robinson (USA)	1.7.1972
9·9	Steve Williams (USA)	21.6.1974
9·9	Silvio Leonard (Cuba)	5.6.1975
9·9	Steve Williams (USA)	16.7.1975
9·9	Steve Williams (USA)	22.8.1975
9·9	Steve Williams (USA)	27.3.1976
9·9	Harvey Glance (USA)	3.4.1976
9·9	Harvey Glance (USA)	1.5.1976
9·9	Don Quarrie (Jamaica)	22.5.1976

100 metres – *contd*
*Fully automatic timing**
sec.

9·95	Jim Hines (USA)	14.10.1968

* Since August 1976 the IAAF has accepted world records in events up to and including 400 m only where timed by an approved, fully automatic electrical timing device.

200 metres (turn)
(First recognized in 1951)
sec.

20·6	Andy Stanfield (USA)	26.5.1951
20·6	Andy Stanfield (USA)	28.6.1952
20·6	Thane Baker (USA)	23.6.1956
20·6	Bobby Morrow (USA)	27.11.1956
20·6	Manfred Germar (Germany)	1.10.1958
20·6	Ray Norton (USA)	19.3.1960
20·6	Ray Norton (USA)	30.4.1960
20·5	Peter Radford (GB)	28.5.1960
20·5	Stone Johnson (USA)	2.7.1960
20·5	Ray Norton (USA)	2.7.1960
20·5	Livio Berruti (Italy)	3.9.1960
20·5	Livio Berruti (Italy)	3.9.1960
20·5	Paul Drayton (USA)	23.6.1962
20·3	Henry Carr (USA)	23.3.1963
20·2	Henry Carr (USA)	4.4.1964
20·0	Tommie Smith (USA)	11.6.1966
19·8	Tommie Smith (USA)	16.10.1968
19·8	Don Quarrie (Jamaica)	3.8.1971
19·8	Don Quarrie (Jamaica)	7.6.1975

Fully automatic timing

19·83	Tommie Smith (USA)	16.10.1968
19·72	Pietro Mennea (Italy)	12.9.1979

400 metres

sec.

47·8	Maxie Long (USA)	29.9.1900
47·4	Ted Meredith (USA)	27.5.1916
47·0	Emerson Spencer (USA)	12.5.1928
46·4	Ben Eastman (USA)	26.3.1932
46·2	Bill Carr (USA)	5.8.1932
46·1	Archie Williams (USA)	19.6.1936
46·0	Rudolf Harbig (Germany)	12.8.1939
46·0	Grover Klemmer (USA)	29.6.1941
46·0	Herb McKenley (Jamaica)	5.6.1948
45·9	Herb McKenley (Jamaica)	2.7.1948
45·8	George Rhoden (Jamaica)	22.8.1950
45·4	Lou Jones (USA)	18.3.1955
45·2	Lou Jones (USA)	30.6.1956
44·9	Otis Davis (USA)	6.9.1960
44·9	Carl Kaufmann (Germany)	6.9.1960
44·9	Adolph Plummer (USA)	25.5.1963
44·9	Mike Larrabee (USA)	12.9.1964
44·5	Tommie Smith (USA)	20.5.1967
44·1	Larry James (USA)	14.9.1968
43·8	Lee Evans (USA)	18.10.1968

Fully automatic timing

43·86	Lee Evans (USA)	18.10.1968

800 metres

min. sec.

1	51·9	Ted Meredith (USA)	8.7.1912
1	51·6	Otto Peltzer (Germany)	3.7.1926
1	50·6	Sera Martin (France)	14.7.1928
1	49·8	Tom Hampson (GB)	2.8.1932
1	49·8	Ben Eastman (USA)	16.6.1934
1	49·7	Glenn Cunningham (USA)	20.8.1936
1	49·6	Elroy Robinson (USA)	11.7.1937

800 metres – *contd*

min. sec.

1	48·4	Sydney Wooderson (GB)	20.8.1938
1	46·6	Rudolf Harbig (Germany)	15.7.1939
1	45·7	Roger Moens (Belgium)	3.8.1955
1	44·3	Peter Snell (NZ)	3.2.1962
1	44·3	Ralph Doubell (Australia)	15.10.1968
1	44·3	Dave Wottle (USA)	1.7.1972
1	43·7	Marcello Fiasconaro (Italy)	27.6.1973
1	43·5	Alberto Juantorena (Cuba)	25.7.1976
1	43·4	Alberto Juantorena (Cuba)	21.8.1977
1	42·4	Sebastian Coe (GB)	5.7.1979

1,500 metres

min. sec.

3	55·8	Abel Kiviat (USA)	8.6.1912
3	54·7	John Zander (Sweden)	5.8.1917
3	52·6	Paavo Nurmi (Finland)	19.6.1924
3	51·0	Otto Peltzer (Germany)	11.9.1926
3	49·2	Jules Ladoumegue (France)	5.10.1930
3	49·2	Luigi Beccali (Italy)	9.9.1933
3	49·0	Luigi Beccali (Italy)	17.9.1933
3	48·8	Bill Bonthron (USA)	30.6.1934
3	47·8	Jack Lovelock (NZ)	6.8.1936
3	47·6	Gunder Haegg (Sweden)	10.8.1941
3	45·8	Gunder Haegg (Sweden)	17.7.1942
3	45·0	Arne Andersson (Sweden)	17.8.1943
3	43·0	Gunder Haegg (Sweden)	7.7.1944
3	43·0	Lennart Strand (Sweden)	15.7.1947
3	43·0	Werner Lueg (Germany)	29.6.1952
3	42·8	Wes Santee (USA)	4.6.1954
3	41·8	John Landy (Australia)	21.6.1954
3	40·8	Sandor Iharos (Hungary)	28.7.1955
3	40·8	Laszlo Tabori (Hungary)	6.9.1955

1,500 metres – *contd*

min. sec.

3	40·8	Gunnar Nielsen (Denmark)	6.9.1955
3	40·6	Istvan Rozsavolgyi (Hungary)	3.8.1956
3	40·2	Olavi Salsola (Finland)	11.7.1957
3	40·2	Olavi Salonen (Finland)	11.7.1957
3	38·1	Stanislav Jungwirth (Czechoslovakia)	12.7.1957
3	36·0	Herb Elliott (Australia)	28.8.1958
3	35·6	Herb Elliott (Australia)	6.9.1960
3	33·1	Jim Ryun (USA)	8.7.1967
3	32·2	Filbert Bayi (Tanzania)	2.2.1974
3	32·1	Sebastian Coe (GB)	15.8.1979

1 mile

min. sec.

4	14·4	John Paul Jones (USA)	31.5.1913
4	12·6	Norman Taber (USA)	16.7.1915
4	10·4	Paavo Nurmi (Finland)	23.8.1923
4	09·2	Jules Ladoumegue (France)	4.10.1931
4	07·6	Jack Lovelock (NZ)	15.7.1933
4	06·8	Glenn Cunningham (USA)	16.6.1934
4	06·4	Sydney Wooderson (GB)	28.8.1937
4	06·2	Gunder Haegg (Sweden)	1.7.1942
4	06·2	Arne Andersson (Sweden)	10.7.1942
4	04·6	Gunder Haegg (Sweden)	4.9.1942
4	02·6	Arne Andersson (Sweden)	1.7.1943
4	01·6	Arne Andersson (Sweden)	18.7.1944
4	01·4	Gunder Haegg (Sweden)	17.7.1945
3	59·4	Roger Bannister (GB)	6.5.1954
3	58.0	John Landy (Australia)	21.6.1954
3	57·2	Derek Ibbotson (GB)	19.7.1957
3	54·5	Herb Elliott (Australia)	6.8.1958
3	54·4	Peter Snell (NZ)	27.1.1962

1 mile – *contd*
min. sec.

3	54·1	Peter Snell (NZ)	17.11.1964
3	53·6	Michel Jazy (France)	9.6.1965
3	51·3	Jim Ryun (USA)	17.7.1966
3	51·1	Jim Ryun (USA)	23.6.1967
3	51·0	Filbert Bayi (Tanzania)	17.5.1975
3	49·4	John Walker (NZ)	12.8.1975
3	49·0	Sebastian Coe (GB)	17.7.1979

5,000 metres
min. sec.

14	36·6	Hannes Kolehmainen (Finland)	10.7.1912
14	35·4	Paavo Nurmi (Finland)	12.9.1922
14	28·2	Paavo Nurmi (Finland)	19.6.1924
14	17·0	Lauri Lehtinen (Finland)	19.6.1932
14	08·8	Taisto Maki (Finland)	16.6.1939
13	58·2	Gunder Haegg (Sweden)	20.9.1942
13	57·2	Emil Zatopek (Czechoslovakia)	30.5.1954
13	56·6	Vladimir Kuts (USSR)	29.8.1954
13	51·6	Chris Chataway (GB)	13.10.1954
13	51·2	Vladimir Kuts (USSR)	23.10.1954
13	50·8	Sandor Iharos (Hungary)	10.9.1955
13	46·8	Vladimir Kuts (USSR)	18.9.1955
13	40·6	Sandor Iharos (Hungary)	23.10.1955
13	36·8	Gordon Pirie (GB)	19.6.1956
13	35·0	Vladimir Kuts (USSR)	13.10.1957
13	34·8	Ron Clarke (Australia)	16.1.1965
13	33·6	Ron Clarke (Australia)	1.2.1965
13	25·8	Ron Clarke (Australia)	4.6.1965
13	24·2	Kipchoge Keino (Kenya)	30.11.1965
13	16·6	Ron Clarke (Australia)	5.7.1966
13	16·4	Lasse Viren (Finland)	14.9.1972
13	13·0	Emiel Puttemans (Belgium)	20.9.1972

5,000 metres – *contd*
min. sec.

13	12·9	Dick Quax (NZ)	5.7.1977
13	08·4	Henry Rono (Kenya)	8.4.1978

10,000 metres
min. sec.

30	58·8	Jean Bouin (France)	16.11.1911
30	40·2	Paavo Nurmi (Finland)	22.6.1921
30	35·4	Ville Ritola (Finland)	25.5.1924
30	23·2	Ville Ritola (Finland)	6.7.1924
30	06·2	Paavo Nurmi (Finland)	31.8.1924
30	05·6	Ilmari Salminen (Finland)	18.7.1937
30	02·0	Taisto Maki (Finland)	29.9.1938
29	52·6	Taisto Maki (Finland)	17.9.1939
29	35·4	Viljo Heino (Finland)	25.8.1944
29	28·2	Emil Zatopek (Czechoslovakia)	11.6.1949
29	27·2	Viljo Heino (Finland)	1.9.1949
29	21·2	Emil Zatopek (Czechoslovakia)	22.10.1949
29	02·6	Emil Zatopek (Czechoslovakia)	4.8.1950
29	01·6	Emil Zatopek (Czechoslovakia)	1.11.1953
28	54·2	Emil Zatopek (Czechoslovakia)	1.6.1954
28	42·8	Sandor Iharos (Hungary)	15.7.1956
28	30·4	Vladimir Kuts (USSR)	11.9.1956
28	18·8	Pyotr Bolotnikov (USSR)	15.10.1960
28	18·2	Pyotr Bolotnikov (USSR)	11.8.1962
28	15·6	Ron Clarke (Australia)	18.12.1963
27	39·4	Ron Clarke (Australia)	14.7.1965
27	38·4	Lasse Viren (Finland)	3.9.1972
27	30·8	David Bedford (GB)	13.7.1973
27	30·5	Samson Kimobwa (Kenya)	30.6.1977
27	22·4	Henry Rono (Kenya)	13.5.1978

3,000 metres steeplechase
(First recognized in 1954)
min. sec.

8 49·6	Sandor Rozsnyoi (Hungary)	28.8.1954
8 47·8	Pentti Karvonen (Finland)	1.7.1955
8 45·4	Pentti Karvonen (Finland)	15.7.1955
8 45·4	Vasiliy Vlasenko (USSR)	18.8.1955
8 41·2	Jerzy Chromik (Poland)	31.8.1955
8 40·2	Jerzy Chromik (Poland)	11.9.1955
8 39·8	Semyon Rzhishchin (USSR)	14.8.1956
8 35·6	Sandor Rozsnyoi (Hungary)	16.9.1956
8 35·6	Semyon Rzhishchin (USSR)	21.7.1958
8 32·0	Jerzy Chromik (Poland)	2.8.1958
8 31·4	Zdzislaw Krzyszkowiak (Poland)	26.6.1960
8 31·2	Grigoriy Taran (USSR)	28.5.1961
8 30·4	Zdzislaw Krzyszkowiak (Poland)	10.8.1961
8 29·6	Gaston Roelants (Belgium)	7.9.1963
8 26·4	Gaston Roelants (Belgium)	7.8.1965
8 24·2	Jouko Kuha (Finland)	17.7.1968
8 22·2	Vladimir Dudin (USSR)	19.8.1969
8 22·0	Kerry O'Brien (Australia)	4.7.1970
8 20·8	Anders Garderud (Sweden)	14.9.1972
8 19·8	Ben Jipcho (Kenya)	19.6.1973
8 14·0	Ben Jipcho (Kenya)	27.6.1973
8 10·4	Anders Garderud (Sweden)	25.6.1975
8 09·8	Anders Garderud (Sweden)	1.7.1975
8 08·0	Anders Garderud (Sweden)	28.7.1976
8 05·4	Henry Rono (Kenya)	13.5.1978

110 metres hurdles
sec.

15·0	Forrest Smithson (USA)	25.7.1908
14·8	Earl Thomson (Canada)	18.8.1920
14·8	Sten Pettersson (Sweden)	18.9.1927

110 metres hurdles – *contd*

sec.

14·6	George Weightman-Smith (S. Africa)	31.7.1928
14·4	Eric Wennstrom (Sweden)	25.8.1929
14·4	Bengt Sjostedt (Finland)	5.9.1931
14·4	Percy Beard (USA)	23.6.1932
14·4	Jack Keller (USA)	16.7.1932
14·4	George Saling (USA)	2.8.1932
14·4	John Morriss (USA)	12.8.1933
14·4	John Morriss (USA)	8.9.1933
14·3	Percy Beard (USA)	26.7.1934
14·2	Percy Beard (USA)	6.8.1934
14·2	Al Moreau (USA)	2.8.1935
14·1	Forrest Towns (USA)	19.6.1936
14·1	Forrest Towns (USA)	6.8.1936
13·7	Forrest Towns (USA)	27.8.1936
13·7	Fred Wolcott (USA)	29.6.1941
13·6	Dick Attlesey (USA)	24.6.1950
13·5	Dick Attlesey (USA)	10.7.1950
13·4	Jack Davis (USA)	22.6.1956
13·2	Martin Lauer (Germany)	7.7.1959
13·2	Lee Calhoun (USA)	21.8.1960
13·2	Earl McCullouch (USA)	16.7.1967
13·2	Willie Davenport (USA)	4.7.1969
13·2	Rod Milburn (USA)	7.9.1972
13·1	Rod Milburn (USA)	6.7.1973
13·1	Rod Milburn (USA)	22.7.1973
13·1	Guy Drut (France)	23.7.1975
13·0	Guy Drut (France)	22.8.1975

Fully automatic timing

13·24	Rod Milburn (USA)	7.9.1972
13·21	Alejandro Casanas (Cuba)	21.8.1977
13·16	Renaldo Nehemiah (USA)	14.4.1979
13·00	Renaldo Nehemiah (USA)	6.5.1979

400 metres hurdles
sec.

55·0	Charles Bacon (USA)	22.7.1908
54·2	John Norton (USA)	26.6.1920
54·0	Frank Loomis (USA)	16.8.1920
53·8	Sten Pettersson (Sweden)	4.10.1925
52·6	John Gibson (USA)	2.7.1927
52·0	Morgan Taylor (USA)	4.7.1928
52·0	Glenn Hardin (USA)	1.8.1932
51·8	Glenn Hardin (USA)	30.6.1934
50·6	Glenn Hardin (USA)	26.7.1934
50·4	Yuriy Lituyev (USSR)	20.9.1953
49·5	Glenn Davis (USA)	29.6.1956
49·2	Glenn Davis (USA)	6.8.1958
49·2	Salvatore Morale (Italy)	14.9.1962
49·1	Rex Cawley (USA)	13.9.1964
48·8	Geoff Vanderstock (USA)	11.9.1968
48·1	David Hemery (GB)	15.10.1968
47·8	John Akii-Bua (Uganda)	2.9.1972

Fully automatic timing

47·82	John Akii-Bua (Uganda)	2.9.1972
47·64	Edwin Moses (USA)	25.7.1976
47·45	Edwin Moses (USA)	11.6.1977

4 × 100 metres relay
sec.

42·3	Germany	8.7.1912
42·2	USA	22.8.1920
42·0	Great Britain	12.7.1924
42·0	Netherlands	12.7.1924
41·0	USA	13.7.1924
41·0	Newark AC (USA)	4.7.1927
41·0	Sport Club, Eintracht (Germany)	10.6.1928

4 × 100 metres relay – *contd*

sec.

41·0	USA	5.8.1928
40·8	Germany	2.9.1928
40·8	Sport Club, Charlottenburg (Germany)	22.7.1929
40·8	Univ. of S. California (USA)	9.5.1931
40·6	Germany	14.6.1932
40·0	USA	7.8.1932
39·8	USA	9.8.1936
39·5	USA	1.12.1956
39·5	Germany	29.8.1958
39·5	Germany	7.9.1960
39·5	Germany	8.9.1960
39·1	USA	15.7.1961
39·0	USA	21.10.1964
38·6	Univ. of S. California (USA)	17.6.1967
38·6	Jamaica	19.10.1968
38·3	Jamaica	19.10.1968
38·2	USA	20.10.1968
38·2	USA	10.9.1972

Fully automatic timing

38·19	USA	10.9.1972
38·03	USA	3.9.1977

4 × 400 metres relay

min. sec.

3	18·2	USA	4.9.1911
3	16·6	USA	15.7.1912
3	16·0	USA	13.7.1924
3	14·2	USA	5.8.1928
3	13·4	USA	11.8.1928
3	12·6	Stanford Univ. (USA)	8.5.1931
3	08·2	USA	7.8.1932

4 × 400 metres relay – *contd*

min. sec.

3 03·9	Jamaica	27.7.1952
3 02·2	USA	8.9.1960
3 00·7	USA	21.10.1964
2 59·6	USA	24.7.1966
2 56·2	USA	20.10.1968

High jump

metres

2·00	George Horine (USA)	18.5.1912
2·01	Edward Beeson (USA)	2.5.1914
2·03	Harold Osborn (USA)	27.5.1924
2·04	Walter Marty (USA)	13.5.1933
2·06	Walter Marty (USA)	28.4.1934
2·07	Cornelius Johnson (USA)	12.7.1936
2·07	David Albritton (USA)	12.7.1936
2·09	Mel Walker (USA)	12.8.1937
2·11	Les Steers (USA)	17.6.1941
2·12	Walter Davis (USA)	27.6.1953
2·15	Charles Dumas (USA)	29.6.1956
2·16	Yuriy Styepanov (USSR)	13.7.1957
2·17	John Thomas (USA)	30.4.1960
2·17	John Thomas (USA)	21.5.1960
2·18	John Thomas (USA)	24.6.1960
2·22	John Thomas (USA)	1.7.1960
2·23	Valeriy Brumel (USSR)	18.6.1961
2·24	Valeriy Brumel (USSR)	16.7.1961
2·25	Valeriy Brumel (USSR)	31.8.1961
2·26	Valeriy Brumel (USSR)	22.7.1962
2·27	Valeriy Brumel (USSR)	29.9.1962
2·28	Valeriy Brumel (USSR)	21.7.1963
2·29	Pat Matzdorf (USA)	3.7.1971
2·30	Dwight Stones (USA)	11.7.1973

High jump – *contd*

metres

2·31	Dwight Stones (USA)	5.6.1976
2·32	Dwight Stones (USA)	4.8.1976
2·33	Vladimir Yashchenko (USSR)	3.7.1977
2·34	Vladimir Yashchenko (USSR)	16.6.1978

Note indoors

2·35	Vladimir Yashchenko (USSR)	12.3.1978

Pole vault

metres

4·02	Marc Wright (USA)	8.6.1912
4·09	Frank Foss (USA)	20.8.1920
4·12	Charles Hoff (Norway)	3.9.1922
4·21	Charles Hoff (Norway)	22.7.1923
4·23	Charles Hoff (Norway)	13.8.1925
4·25	Charles Hoff (Norway)	27.9.1925
4·27	Sabin Carr (USA)	27.5.1927
4·30	Lee Barnes (USA)	28.4.1928
4·37	Bill Graber (USA)	16.7.1932
4·39	Keith Brown (USA)	1.6.1935
4·43	George Varoff (USA)	4.7.1936
4·54	Bill Sefton (USA)	29.5.1937
4·54	Earle Meadows (USA)	29.5.1937
4·60	Cornelius Warmerdam (USA)	29.6.1940
4·72	Cornelius Warmerdam (USA)	6.6.1941
4·77	Cornelius Warmerdam (USA)	23.5.1942
4·78	Bob Gutowski (USA)	27.4.1957
4·80	Don Bragg (USA)	2.7.1960
4·83	George Davies (USA)	20.5.1961
4·89	John Uelses (USA)	31.3.1962
4·93	Dave Tork (USA)	28.4.1962
4·94	Pentti Nikula (Finland)	22.6.1962
5·00	Brian Sternberg (USA)	27.4.1963

Pole vault – *contd*
metres

5·08	Brian Sternberg (USA)	7.6.1963
5·13	John Pennel (USA)	5.8.1963
5·20	John Pennel (USA)	24.8.1963
5·23	Fred Hansen (USA)	13.6.1964
5·28	Fred Hansen (USA)	25.7.1964
5·32	Bob Seagren (USA)	14.5.1966
5·34	John Pennel (USA)	23.7.1966
5·36	Bob Seagren (USA)	10.6.1967
5·38	Paul Wilson (USA)	23.6.1967
5·41	Bob Seagren (USA)	12.9.1968
5·44	John Pennel (USA)	21.6.1969
5·45	Wolfgang Nordwig (GDR)	17.6.1970
5·46	Wolfgang Nordwig (GDR)	3.9.1970
5·49	Christos Papanicolaou (Greece)	24.10.1970
5·51	Kjell Isaksson (Sweden)	8.4.1972
5·54	Kjell Isaksson (Sweden)	15.4.1972
5·55	Kjell Isaksson (Sweden)	12.6.1972
5·63	Bob Seagren (USA)	2.7.1972
5·65	Dave Roberts (USA)	28.3.1975
5·67	Earl Bell (USA)	29.5.1976
5·70	Dave Roberts (USA)	22.6.1976

Long jump
metres

7·61	Peter O'Connor (GB/Ireland)	5.8.1901
7·69	Edwin Gourdin (USA)	23.7.1921
7·76	Robert LeGendre (USA)	7.7.1924
7·89	William de Hart Hubbard (USA)	13.6.1925
7·90	Edward Hamm (USA)	7.7.1928
7·93	Sylvio Cator (Haiti)	9.9.1928
7·98	Chuhei Nambu (Japan)	27.10.1931
8·13	Jesse Owens (USA)	25.5.1935

Long jump – *contd*

metres

8·21	Ralph Boston (USA)	12.8.1960
8·24	Ralph Boston (USA)	27.5.1961
8·28	Ralph Boston (USA)	16.7.1961
8·31	Igor Ter-Ovanesyan (USSR)	10.6.1962
8·31	Ralph Boston (USA)	15.8.1964
8·34	Ralph Boston (USA)	12.9.1964
8·35	Ralph Boston (USA)	29.5.1965
8·35	Igor Ter-Ovanesyan (USSR)	19.10.1967
8·90	Bob Beamon (USA)	18.10.1968

Triple jump

metres

15·52	Daniel Ahearn (USA)	30.5.1911
15·52	Anthony Winter (Australia)	12.7.1924
15·58	Mikio Oda (Japan)	27.10.1931
15·72	Chuhei Nambu (Japan)	4.8.1932
15·78	Jack Metcalfe (Australia)	14.12.1935
16·00	Naoto Tajima (Japan)	6.8.1936
16·00	Adhemar da Silva (Brazil)	3.12.1950
16·01	Adhemar da Silva (Brazil)	30.9.1951
16·12	Adhemar da Silva (Brazil)	23.7.1952
16·22	Adhemar da Silva (Brazil)	23.7.1952
16·23	Leonid Shcherbakov (USSR)	19.7.1953
16·56	Adhemar da Silva (Brazil)	16.3.1955
16·59	Olyeg Ryakhovskiy (USSR)	28.7.1958
16·70	Olyeg Fedoseyev (USSR)	3.5.1959
17·03	Jozef Szmidt (Poland)	5.8.1960
17·10	Giuseppe Gentile (Italy)	16.10.1968
17·22	Giuseppe Gentile (Italy)	17.10.1968
17·23	Viktor Saneyev (USSR)	17.10.1968
17·27	Nelson Prudencio (Brazil)	17.10.1968
17·39	Viktor Saneyev (USSR)	17.10.1968

Triple jump – *contd*
metres

17·40	Pedro Perez (Cuba)	5.8.1971
17·44	Viktor Saneyev (USSR)	17.10.1972
17·89	Joao de Oliveira (Brazil)	15.10.1975

Shot
metres

15·54	Ralph Rose (USA)	21.8.1909
15·79	Emil Hirschfeld (Germany)	6.5.1928
15·87	John Kuck (USA)	29.7.1928
16·04	Emil Hirschfeld (Germany)	26.8.1928
16·04	Frantisek Douda (Czechoslovakia)	4.10.1931
16·05	Zygmunt Heljasz (Poland)	29.6.1932
16·16	Leo Sexton (USA)	27.8.1932
16·20	Frantisek Douda (Czechoslovakia)	24.9.1932
16·48	John Lyman (USA)	21.4.1934
16·80	Jack Torrance (USA)	27.4.1934
16·89	Jack Torrance (USA)	30.6.1934
17·40	Jack Torrance (USA)	5.8.1934
17·68	Charles Fonville (USA)	17.4.1948
17·79	Jim Fuchs (USA)	28.7.1949
17·82	Jim Fuchs (USA)	29.4.1950
17·90	Jim Fuchs (USA)	20.8.1950
17·95	Jim Fuchs (USA)	22.8.1950
18·00	Parry O'Brien (USA)	9.5.1953
18·04	Parry O'Brien (USA)	5.6.1953
18·42	Parry O'Brien (USA)	8.5.1954
18·43	Parry O'Brien (USA)	21.5.1954
18·54	Parry O'Brien (USA)	11.6.1954
18·62	Parry O'Brien (USA)	5.5.1956
18·69	Parry O'Brien (USA)	15.6.1956

Shot – *contd*

metres

19·06	Parry O'Brien (USA)	3.9.1956
19·25	Parry O'Brien (USA)	1.11.1956
19·25	Dallas Long (USA)	28.3.1959
19·30	Parry O'Brien (USA)	1.8.1959
19·38	Dallas Long (USA)	5.3.1960
19·45	Bill Nieder (USA)	19.3.1960
19·67	Dallas Long (USA)	26.3.1960
19·99	Bill Nieder (USA)	2.4.1960
20·06	Bill Nieder (USA)	12.8.1960
20·08	Dallas Long (USA)	18.5.1962
20·10	Dallas Long (USA)	4.4.1964
20·20	Dallas Long (USA)	29.5.1964
20·68	Dallas Long (USA)	25.7.1964
21·52	Randy Matson (USA)	8.5.1965
21·78	Randy Matson (USA)	22.4.1967
21·82	Al Feuerbach (USA)	5.5.1973
21·85	Terry Albritton (USA)	21.2.1976
22·00	Aleksandr Baryshnikov (USSR)	10.7.1976
22·15	Udo Beyer (GDR)	6.7.1978

Discus

metres

47·58	James Duncan (USA)	27.5.1912
47·61	Thomas Lieb (USA)	14.9.1924
47·89	Glenn Hartranft (USA)	2.5.1925
48·20	Clarence Houser (USA)	3.4.1926
49·90	Eric Krenz (USA)	9.3.1929
51·03	Eric Krenz (USA)	17.5.1930
51·73	Paul Jessup (USA)	23.8.1930
52·42	Harald Andersson (Sweden)	25.8.1934
53·10	Willi Schroder (Germany)	28.4.1935
53·26	Archie Harris (USA)	20.6.1941

116

Discus – *contd*

metres

53·34	Adolfo Consolini (Italy)	26.10.1941
54·23	Adolfo Consolini (Italy)	14.4.1946
54·93	Robert Fitch (USA)	8.6.1946
55·33	Adolfo Consolini (Italy)	10.10.1948
56·46	Fortune Gordien (USA)	9.7.1949
56·97	Fortune Gordien (USA)	14.8.1949
57·93	Sim Iness (USA)	20.6.1953
58·10	Fortune Gordien (USA)	11.7.1953
59·28	Fortune Gordien (USA)	22.8.1953
59·91	Edmund Piatkowski (Poland)	14.6.1959
59·91	Rink Babka (USA)	12.8.1960
60·56	Jay Silvester (USA)	11.8.1961
60·72	Jay Silvester (USA)	20.8.1961
61·10	Al Oerter (USA)	18.5.1962
61·64	Vladimir Trusenyov (USSR)	4.6.1962
62·45	Al Oerter (USA)	1.7.1962
62·62	Al Oerter (USA)	27.4.1963
62·94	Al Oerter (USA)	25.4.1964
64·55	Ludvik Danek (Czechoslovakia)	2.8.1964
65·22	Ludvik Danek (Czechoslovakia)	12.10.1965
66·54	Jay Silvester (USA)	25.5.1968
68·40	Jay Silvester (USA)	18.9.1968
68·40	Ricky Bruch (Sweden)	5.7.1972
68·48	John van Reenan (S. Africa)	14.3.1975
69·08	John Powell (USA)	4.5.1975
69·18	Mac Wilkins (USA)	24.4.1976
69·80	Mac Wilkins (USA)	1.5.1976
70·24	Mac Wilkins (USA)	1.5.1976
70·86	Mac Wilkins (USA)	1.5.1976
71·16	Wolfgang Schmidt (GDR)	9.8.1978

Hammer

metres

57·77	Patrick Ryan (USA)	17.8.1913
59·00	Erwin Blask (Germany)	27.8.1938
59·02	Imre Nemeth (Hungary)	14.7.1948
59·57	Imre Nemeth (Hungary)	4.9.1949
59·88	Imre Nemeth (Hungary)	19.5.1950
60·34	Jozsef Csermak (Hungary)	24.7.1952
61·25	Sverre Strandli (Norway)	14.9.1952
62·36	Sverre Strandli (Norway)	5.9.1953
63·34	Mikhail Krivonosov (USSR)	29.8.1954
64·05	Stanislav Nyenashev (USSR)	12.12.1954
64·33	Mikhail Krivonosov (USSR)	4.8.1955
64·52	Mikhail Krivonosov (USSR)	19.9.1955
65·85	Mikhail Krivonosov (USSR)	25.4.1956
66·38	Mikhail Krivonosov (USSR)	8.7.1956
67·32	Mikhail Krivonosov (USSR)	22.10.1956
68·54	Harold Connolly (USA)	2.11.1956
68·68	Harold Connolly (USA)	20.6.1958
70·33	Harold Connolly (USA)	12.8.1960
70·67	Harold Connolly (USA)	21.7.1962
71·06	Harold Connolly (USA)	29.5.1965
71·26	Harold Connolly (USA)	20.6.1965
73·74	Gyula Zsivotzky (Hungary)	4.9.1965
73·76	Gyula Zsivotzky (Hungary)	14.9.1968
74·52	Romuald Klim (USSR)	15.6.1969
74·68	Anatoliy Bondarchuk (USSR)	20.9.1969
75·48	Anatoliy Bondarchuk (USSR)	12.10.1969
76·40	Walter Schmidt (Germany)	4.9.1971
76·60	Reinhard Theimer (GDR)	4.7.1974
76·66	Aleksey Spiridonov (USSR)	11.9.1974
76·70	Karl-Hans Riehm (Germany)	19.5.1975
77·56	Karl-Hans Riehm (Germany)	19.5.1975
78·50	Karl-Hans Riehm (Germany)	19.5.1975
79·30	Walter Schmidt (Germany)	14.8.1975

Hammer – *contd*
metres
80·14	Boris Zaichuk (USSR)	9.7.1978
80·32	Karl-Hans Riehm (Germany)	6.8.1978

Javelin
metres
62·32	Erik Lemming (Sweden)	29.9.1912
66·10	Jonni Myyra (Finland)	25.8.1919
66·62	Gunnar Lindstrom (Sweden)	12.10.1924
69·88	Eino Penttila (Finland)	8.10.1927
71·01	Erik Lundqvist (Sweden)	15.8.1928
71·57	Matti Jarvinen (Finland)	8.8.1930
71·70	Matti Jarvinen (Finland)	17.8.1930
71·88	Matti Jarvinen (Finland)	31.8.1930
72·93	Matti Jarvinen (Finland)	14.9.1930
74·02	Matti Jarvinen (Finland)	27.6.1932
74·28	Matti Jarvinen (Finland)	25.5.1933
74·61	Matti Jarvinen (Finland)	7.6.1933
76·10	Matti Jarvinen (Finland)	15.6.1933
76·66	Matti Jarvinen (Finland)	7.9.1934
77·23	Matti Jarvinen (Finland)	18.6.1936
77·87	Yrjo Nikkanen (Finland)	25.8.1938
78·70	Yrjo Nikkanen (Finland)	16.10.1938
80·41	Bud Held (USA)	8.8.1953
81·75	Bud Held (USA)	21.5.1955
83·56	Soini Nikkinen (Finland)	24.6.1956
83·66	Janusz Sidlo (Poland)	30.6.1956
85·71	Egil Danielsen (Norway)	26.11.1956
86·04	Al Cantello (USA)	5.6.1959
86·74	Carlo Lievore (Italy)	1.6.1961
87·12	Terje Pedersen (Norway)	1.7.1964
91·72	Terje Pedersen (Norway)	2.9.1964
91·98	Janis Lusis (USSR)	23.6.1968

Javelin – *contd*

metres

92·70	Jorma Kinnunen (Finland)	18.6.1969
93·80	Janis Lusis (USSR)	6.7.1972
94·08	Klaus Wolfermann (Germany)	5.5.1973
94·58	Miklos Nemeth (Hungary)	26.7.1976

Decathlon

100 metres, long jump, shot put, high jump, 400 metres, 110 metres hurdles, discus throw, pole vault, javelin throw, 1,500 metres

1920 Points Tables

7481	Aleksander Klumberg (Estonia)	16/17.9.1922
7710	Harold Osborn (USA)	11/12.7.1924
7821	Paavo Yrjola (Finland)	17/18.7.1926
7995	Paavo Yrjola (Finland)	16/17.7.1927
8053	Paavo Yrjola (Finland)	3/4.8.1928
8255	Akilles Jarvinen (Finland)	19/20.7.1930
8462	James Bausch (USA)	5/6.8.1932
8467	Hans-Heinrich Sievert (Germany)	22/23.7.1933

1934 Points Tables

7824	Hans-Heinrich Sievert (Germany)	7/8.7.1934
7900	Glenn Morris (USA)	7/8.8.1936
8042	Bob Mathias (USA)	29/30.6.1950

1950 Points Tables

7887	Bob Mathias (USA)	25/26.7.1952
7985	Rafer Johnson (USA)	10/11.6.1955
8014	Vasiliy Kuznyetsov (USSR)	17/18.5.1958
8302	Rafer Johnson (USA)	27/28.7.1958
8357	Vasiliy Kuznyetsov (USSR)	16/17.5.1959
8683	Rafer Johnson (USA)	8/9.7.1960

Decathlon – *contd*
1962 Points Tables

8089	Yang Chuan-Kwang (Taiwan)	27/28.4.1963
8230	Russ Hodge (USA)	23/24.7.1966
8319	Kurt Bendlin (Germany)	13/14.5.1967
8417	Bill Toomey (USA)	10/11.12.1969
8456*	Nikolay Avilov (USSR)	7/8.9.1972
8524	Bruce Jenner (USA)	9/10.8.1975
8538	Bruce Jenner (USA)	25/26.6.1976
8617*	Bruce Jenner (USA)	29/30.7.1976

* 1977 Points Tables (electrical timing).

Women

100 metres
sec.

11·7	Stanislawa Walasiewicz (Poland)	26.8.1934
11·6	Stanislawa Walasiewicz (Poland)	1.8.1937
11·5	Fanny Blankers-Koen (Netherlands)	13.6.1948
11·5	Marjorie Jackson (Australia)	22.7.1952
11·4	Marjorie Jackson (Australia)	4.10.1952
11·3	Shirley de la Hunty (Australia)	4.8.1955
11·3	Vera Krepkina (USSR)	13.9.1958
11·3	Wilma Rudolph (USA)	2.9.1960
11·2	Wilma Rudolph (USA)	19.7.1961
11·2	Wyomia Tyus (USA)	15.10.1964
11·1	Irena Kirszenstein (Poland)	9.7.1965
11·1	Wyomia Tyus (USA)	31.7.1965
11·1	Barbara Ferrell (USA)	2.7.1967
11·1	Ludmila Samotyosova (USSR)	15.8.1968
11·1	Irena Szewinska, *née* Kirszenstein (Poland)	14.10.1968

100 metres – *contd*

sec.

11·0	Wyomia Tyus (USA)	15.10.1968
11·0	Chi Cheng (Taiwan)	18.7.1970
11·0	Renate Meissner (GDR)	2.8.1970
11·0	Renate Stecher, *née* Meissner (GDR)	31.7.1971
11·0	Renate Stecher (GDR)	3.6.1972
11·0	Ellen Stropahl (GDR)	15.6.1972
11·0	Eva Gleskova (Czechoslovakia)	1.7.1972
10·9	Renate Stecher (GDR)	7.6.1973
10·8	Renate Stecher (GDR)	20.7.1973

Fully automatic timing

11·08	Wyomia Tyus (USA)	15.10.1968
11·07	Renate Stecher (GDR)	2.9.1972
11·04	Inge Helten (Germany)	13.6.1976
11·01	Annegret Richter (Germany)	25.7.1976
10·88	Marlies Oelsner (GDR)	1.7.1977

200 metres

sec.

23·6	Stanisława Walasiewicz (Poland)	15.8.1935
23·6	Marjorie Jackson (Australia)	25.7.1952
23·4	Marjorie Jackson (Australia)	25.7.1952
23·2	Betty Cuthbert (Australia)	16.9.1956
23·2	Betty Cuthbert (Australia)	7.3.1960
22·9	Wilma Rudolph (USA)	9.7.1960
22·9	Margaret Burvill (Australia)	22.2.1964
22·7	Irena Kirszenstein (Poland)	8.8.1965
22·5	Irena Szewinska, *née* Kirszenstein (Poland)	18.10.1968
22·4	Chi Cheng (Taiwan)	12.7.1970
22·4	Renate Stecher (GDR)	7.9.1972
22·1	Renate Stecher (GDR)	21.7.1973

200 metres – *contd*
Fully automatic timing
sec.

22·21	Irena Szewinska (Poland)	13.6.1974
22·06	Marita Koch (GDR)	28.5.1978
22·02	Marita Koch (GDR)	3.6.1979
21·71	Marita Koch (GDR)	10.6.1979

400 metres
sec.

57·0	Marlene Mathews (Australia)	6.1.1957
57·0	Marise Chamberlain (NZ)	16.2.1957
56·3	Nancy Boyle (Australia)	24.2.1957
55·2	Polina Lazareva (USSR)	10.5.1957
54·0	Maria Itkina (USSR)	8.6.1957
53·6	Maria Itkina (USSR)	6.7.1957
53·4	Maria Itkina (USSR)	12.9.1959
53·4	Maria Itkina (USSR)	14.9.1962
51·9	Sin Kim Dan (N. Korea)	23.10.1962
51·7	Nicole Duclos (France)	18.9.1969
51·7	Colette Besson (France)	18.9.1969
51·0	Marilyn Neufville (Jamaica)	23.7.1970
51·0	Monika Zehrt (GDR)	4.7.1972
49·9	Irena Szewinska (Poland)	22.6.1974

Fully automatic timing

50·14	Riita Salin (Finland)	4.9.1974
49·77	Christine Brehmer (GDR)	9.5.1976
49·75	Irena Szewinska (Poland)	22.6.1976
49·29	Irena Szewinska (Poland)	29.7.1976
49·19	Marita Koch (GDR)	2.7.1978
49·03	Marita Koch (GDR)	19.8.1978
48·94	Marita Koch (GDR)	31.8.1978
48·89	Marita Koch (GDR)	29.7.1979
48·60	Marita Koch (GDR)	4.8.1979

800 metres
min. sec.

2	16·8	Lina Batschauer-Radke (Germany)	2.8.1928
2	15·9	Anna Larsson (Sweden)	28.8.1944
2	14·8	Anna Larsson (Sweden)	19.8.1945
2	13·8	Anna Larsson (Sweden)	30.8.1945
2	13·0	Yevdokiya Vasilyeva (USSR)	17.7.1950
2	12·2	Valentina Pomogayeva (USSR)	26.7.1951
2	12·0	Nina Pletnyova (USSR)	26.8.1951
2	08·5	Nina Pletnyova (USSR)	15.6.1952
2	07·3	Nina Otkalenko, *née* Pletnyova (USSR)	27.8.1953
2	06·6	Nina Otkalenko (USSR)	16.9.1954
2	05·0	Nina Otkalenko (USSR)	24.9.1955
2	04·3	Lyudmila Shevtsova (USSR)	3.7.1960
2	04·3	Lyudmila Shevtsova (USSR)	7.9.1960
2	01·2	Dixie Willis (Australia)	3.3.1962
2	01·1	Ann Packer (GB)	20.10.1964
2	01·0	Judy Pollock (Australia)	28.6.1967
2	00·5	Vera Nikolic (Yugoslavia)	20.7.1968
1	59·5	Hildegard Falck (Germany)	11.7.1971
1	57·5	Svetla Zlateva (Bulgaria)	24.8.1973
1	56·0	Valentina Gerasimova (USSR)	12.6.1976
1	54·9	Tatyana Kazankina (USSR)	26.7.1976

1,500 metres
min. sec.

4	17·3	Anne Smith (GB)	3.6.1967
4	15·6	Maria Gommers (Netherlands)	24.10.1967
4	12·4	Paola Pigni (Italy)	2.7.1969
4	10·7	Jaroslava Jehlickova (Czechoslovakia)	20.9.1969
4	09·6	Karin Burneleit (GDR)	15.8.1971
4	06·9	Lyudmila Bragina (USSR)	18.7.1972

1,500 metres – *contd*
min. sec.

4 06·5	Lyudmila Bragina (USSR)	4.9.1972
4 05·1	Lyudmila Bragina (USSR)	7.9.1972
4 01·4	Lyudmila Bragina (USSR)	9.9.1972
3 56·0	Tatyana Kazankina (USSR)	28.6.1976

100 metres hurdles
sec.

13·3	Karin Balzer (GDR)	20.6.1969
13·3	Teresa Sukniewicz (Poland)	20.6.1969
13·0	Karin Balzer (GDR)	27.7.1969
12·9	Karin Balzer (GDR)	5.9.1969
12·8	Teresa Sukniewicz (Poland)	20.6.1970
12·8	Chi Cheng (Taiwan)	12.7.1970
12·7	Karin Balzer (GDR)	26.7.1970
12·7	Teresa Sukniewicz (Poland)	20.9.1970
12·7	Karin Balzer (GDR)	25.7.1971
12·6	Karin Balzer (GDR)	31.7.1971
12·5	Annelie Ehrhardt (GDR)	15.6.1972
12·5	Pam Ryan (Australia)	28.6.1972
12·3	Annelie Ehrhardt (GDR)	22.7.1973

Fully automatic timing

12·59	Annelie Ehrhardt (GDR)	8.9.1972
12·48	Grazyna Rabsztyn (Poland)	10.6.1978
12·48	Grazyna Rabsztyn (Poland)	18.6.1979

4 × 100 metres relay
sec.

46·4	Germany	8.8.1936
46·1	Australia	27.7.1952
45·9	USA	27.7.1952
45·9	Germany	27.7.1952

4 × 100 metres – *contd*

sec.

45·6	USSR	20.9.1953
45·6	USSR	11.9.1955
45·2	USSR	27.7.1956
45·1	Germany	30.9.1956
44·9	Australia	1.12.1956
44·9	Germany	1.12.1956
44·5	Australia	1.12.1956
44·4	USA	7.9.1960
44·3	USA	15.7.1961
43·9	USA	21.10.1964
43·9	USSR	16.8.1968
43·6	USSR	27.9.1968
43·4	USA	19.10.1968
43·4	Netherlands	19.10.1968
42·8	USA	20.10.1968
42·8	Germany	10.9.1972
42·6	GDR	1.9.1973
42·6	GDR	24.8.1974
42·5	GDR	8.9.1974

Fully automatic timing

42·51	GDR	8.9.1974
42·50	GDR	29.5.1976
42·27	GDR.	19.8.1978
42·10	GDR	10.6.1979
42·09	GDR	4.8.1979

4 × 400 metres relay

min. sec.

3	47·4	Moscow (USSR)	30.5.1969
3	43·2	Latvia (USSR)	1.6.1969
3	37·6	Great Britain	22.6.1969
3	34·2	France	6.7.1969

4 × 400 metres relay – *contd*

min. sec.

3	33·9	Germany	19.9.1969
3	30·8	Great Britain	20.9.1969
3	30·8	France	20.9.1969
3	29·3	GDR	15.8.1971
3	28·8	GDR	5.7.1972
3	28·5	GDR	9.9.1972
3	23·0	GDR	10.9.1972
3	19·2	GDR	31.7.1976

High jump

metres

1·65	Jean Shiley (USA)	7.8.1932
1·65	Mildred Didrikson (USA)	7.8.1932
1·66	Dorothy Odam (GB)	29.5.1939
1·66	Esther Van Heerden (S. Africa)	29.3.1941
1·66	Ilsebill Pfenning (Switzerland)	27.7.1941
1·71	Fanny Blankers-Koen (Netherlands)	30.5.1943
1·72	Sheila Lerwill (GB)	7.7.1951
1·73	Aleksandra Chudina (USSR)	22.5.1954
1·74	Thelma Hopkins (GB)	5.5.1956
1·75	Iolanda Balas (Romania)	14.7.1956
1·76	Mildred McDaniel (USA)	1.12.1956
1·76	Iolanda Balas (Romania)	13.10.1957
1·77	Cheng Feng-Yung (China)	17.11.1957
1·78	Iolanda Balas (Romania)	7.6.1958
1·80	Iolanda Balas (Romania)	22.6.1958
1·81	Iolanda Balas (Romania)	31.7.1958
1·82	Iolanda Balas (Romania)	4.10.1958
1·83	Iolanda Balas (Romania)	18.10.1958
1·84	Iolanda Balas (Romania)	21.9.1959
1·85	Iolanda Balas (Romania)	6.6.1960

High jump – *contd*

metres

1·86	Iolanda Balas (Romania)	10.7.1960
1·87	Iolanda Balas (Romania)	15.4.1961
1·88	Iolanda Balas (Romania)	18.6.1961
1·90	Iolanda Balas (Romania)	8.7.1961
1·91	Iolanda Balas (Romania)	16.7.1961
1·92	Ilona Gusenbauer (Austria)	4.9.1971
1·92	Ulrike Meyfarth (Germany)	4.9.1972
1·94	Yordanka Blagoyeva (Bulgaria)	24.9.1972
1·94	Rosemarie Witschas (GDR)	24.8.1974
1·95	Rosemarie Witschas (GDR)	8.9.1974
1·96	Rosemarie Ackermann (*née* Witschas) (GDR)	8.5.1976
1·96	Rosemarie Ackermann (GDR)	3.7.1977
1·97	Rosemarie Ackermann (GDR)	14.8.1977
1·97	Rosemarie Ackermann (GDR)	26.8.1977
2·00	Rosemarie Ackermann (GDR)	26.8.1977
2·01	Sara Simeoni (Italy)	4.8.1978
2·01	Sara Simeoni (Italy)	31.8.1978

Long jump

metres

5·98	Kinue Hitomi (Japan)	20.5.1928
6·12	Christel Schulz (Germany)	30.7.1939
6·25	Fanny Blankers-Koen (Netherlands)	19.9.1943
6·28	Yvette Williams (NZ)	20.2.1954
6·28	Galina Vinogradova (USSR)	11.9.1955
6·31	Galina Vinogradova (USSR)	18.11.1955
6·35	Elzbieta Krzesinska (Poland)	20.8.1956
6·35	Elzbieta Krzesinska (Poland)	27.11.1956
6·40	Hildrun Claus (GDR)	7.8.1960
6·42	Hildrun Claus (GDR)	23.6.1961

Long jump – *contd*
metres

6·48	Tatyana Shchelkanova (USSR)	16.7.1961
6·53	Tatyana Shchelkanova (USSR)	10.6.1962
6·70	Tatyana Shchelkanova (USSR)	4.7.1964
6·76	Mary Rand (GB)	14.10.1964
6·82	Viorica Viscopoleanu (Romania)	14.10.1968
6·84	Heide Rosendahl (Germany)	3.9.1970
6·92	Angela Voigt (GDR)	9.5.1976
6·99	Sigrun Siegl (GDR)	19.5.1976
7·07	Vilma Bardauskiene (USSR)	18.8.1978
7·09	Vilma Bardauskiene (USSR)	29.8.1978

Shot
metres

14·38	Gisela Mauermayer (Germany)	15.7.1934
14·59	Tatyana Sevryukova (USSR)	4.8.1948
14·86	Klavdiya Tochonova (USSR)	30.10.1949
15·02	Anna Andreyeva (USSR)	9.11.1950
15·28	Galina Zybina (USSR)	26.7.1952
15·37	Galina Zybina (USSR)	20.9.1952
15·42	Galina Zybina (USSR)	1.10.1952
16·20	Galina Zybina (USSR)	9.10.1953
16·28	Galina Zybina (USSR)	14.9.1954
16·29	Galina Zybina (USSR)	5.9.1955
16·67	Galina Zybina (USSR)	15.11.1955
16·76	Galina Zybina (USSR)	13.10.1956
17·25	Tamara Press (USSR)	26.4.1959
17·42	Tamara Press (USSR)	16.7.1960
17·78	Tamara Press (USSR)	13.8.1960
18·55	Tamara Press (USSR)	10.6.1962
18·55	Tamara Press (USSR)	12.9.1962
18·59	Tamara Press (USSR)	19.9.1965
18·67	Nadyezhda Chizhova (USSR)	28.4.1968

Shot – *contd*
metres

18·87	Margitta Gummel (GDR)	22.9.1968
19·07	Margitta Gummel (GDR)	20.10.1968
19·61	Margitta Gummel (GDR)	20.10.1968
19·72	Nadyezhda Chizhova (USSR)	30.5.1969
20·09	Nadyezhda Chizhova (USSR)	13.7.1969
20·10	Margitta Gummel (GDR)	11.9.1969
20·10	Nadyezhda Chizhova (USSR)	16.9.1969
20·43	Nadyezhda Chizhova (USSR)	16.9.1969
20·43	Nadyezhda Chizhova (USSR)	29.8.1971
20·63	Nadyezhda Chizhova (USSR)	19.5.1972
21·03	Nadyezhda Chizhova (USSR)	7.9.1972
21·20	Nadyezhda Chizhova (USSR)	28.8.1973
21·60	Marianne Adam (GDR)	6.8.1975
21·67	Marianne Adam (GDR)	30.5.1976
21·87	Ivanka Khristova (Bulgaria)	3.7.1976
21·89	Ivanka Khristova (Bulgaria)	4.7.1976
21·99	Helena Fibingerova (Czechoslovakia)	26.9.1976
22·32	Helena Fibingerova (Czechoslovakia)	20.8.1977

Indoors

22·50	Helena Fibingerova (Czechoslovakia)	19.2.1977

Discus
metres

48·31	Gisela Mauermayer (Germany)	11.7.1936
53·25	Nina Dumbadze (USSR)	8.8.1948
53·37	Nina Dumbadze (USSR)	27.5.1951
53·61	Nina Romashkova (USSR)	9.8.1952
57·04	Nina Dumbadze (USSR)	18.10.1952
57·15	Tamara Press (USSR)	12.9.1960

Discus – *contd*
metres

57·43	Tamara Press (USSR)	15.7.1961
58·06	Tamara Press (USSR)	1.9.1961
58·98	Tamara Press (USSR)	20.9.1961
59·29	Tamara Press (USSR)	18.5.1963
59·70	Tamara Press (USSR)	11.8.1965
61·26	Liesel Westermann (Germany)	5.11.1967
61·64	Christine Spielberg (GDR)	26.5.1968
62·54	Liesel Westermann (Germany)	24.7.1968
62·70	Liesel Westermann (Germany)	18.6.1969
63·96	Liesel Westermann (Germany)	27.9.1969
64·22	Faina Melnik (USSR)	12.8.1971
64·88	Faina Melnik (USSR)	4.9.1971
65·42	Faina Melnik (USSR)	31.5.1972
65·48	Faina Melnik (USSR)	24.6.1972
66·76	Faina Melnik (USSR)	4.8.1972
67·32	Argentina Menis (Romania)	23.9.1972
67·44	Faina Melnik (USSR)	25.5.1973
67·58	Faina Melnik (USSR)	10.7.1973
69·48	Faina Melnik (USSR)	7.9.1973
69·90	Faina Melnik (USSR)	27.5.1974
70·20	Faina Melnik (USSR)	20.8.1975
70·50	Faina Melnik (USSR)	24.4.1976
70·72	Evelin Jahl (GDR)	12.8.1978

Javelin
metres

46·74	Nan Gindele (USA)	18.6.1932
47·24	Anneliese Steinheuer (Germany)	21.6.1942
48·21	Herma Bauma (Austria)	29.6.1947
48·63	Herma Bauma (Austria)	12.9.1948
49·59	Natalya Smirnitskaya (USSR)	25.7.1949
53·41	Natalya Smirnitskaya (USSR)	5.8.1949

Javelin – *contd*

metres

53·56	Nadyezhda Konyayeva (USSR)	5.2.1954
55·11	Nadyezhda Konyayeva (USSR)	22.5.1954
55·48	Nadyezhda Konyayeva (USSR)	6.8.1954
55·73	Dana Zatopkova (Czechoslovakia)	1.6.1958
57·40	Anna Pazera (Australia)	24.7.1958
57·49	Birute Zalogaitite (USSR)	30.10.1958
57·92	Elvira Ozolina (USSR)	3.5.1960
59·55	Elvira Ozolina (USSR)	4.6.1960
59·78	Elvira Ozolina (USSR)	3.7.1963
62·40	Yelena Gorchakova (USSR)	16.10.1964
62·70	Ewa Gryziecka (Poland)	11.6.1972
65·06	Ruth Fuchs (GDR)	11.6.1972
66·10	Ruth Fuchs (GDR)	7.9.1973
67·22	Ruth Fuchs (GDR)	3.9.1974
69·12	Ruth Fuchs (GDR)	10.7.1976
69·32	Kate Schmidt (USA)	11.9.1977
69·52	Ruth Fuchs (GDR)	13.6.1979

Pentathlon

Shot, high jump, 200 metres, 80 metres hurdles, long jump

1954 Points Tables

4692	Fanny Blankers-Koen (Netherlands)	15/16.9.1951
4704	Aleksandra Chudina (USSR)	8/9.8.1953
4747	Nina Martynenko (USSR)	6/7.7.1955
4750	Aleksandra Chudina (USSR)	6/7.7.1955
4767	Nina Vinogradova (USSR)	11/12.8.1956
4846	Galina Bystrova (USSR)	15/16.10.1957
4872	Galina Bystrova (USSR)	1/2.11.1958
4880	Irina Press (USSR)	13/14.9.1959
4902	Irina Press (USSR)	21/22.5.1960
4959	Irina Press (USSR)	25/26.6.1960

Pentathlon – *contd*
1954 Points Table

4972	Irina Press (USSR)	17/18.10.1960
5137	Irina Press (USSR)	8/9.10.1961
5246	Irina Press (USSR)	16/17.10.1964

100 metres hurdles, shot, high jump, long jump, 200 metres

5352	Liese Prokop (Austria)	4/5.10.1969
5406	Burglinde Pollak (GDR)	5/6.9.1970

1971 Points Tables

4801	Mary Peters (GB)	2/3.9.1972
4831	Burglinde Pollak (GDR)	12.8.1973
4932	Burglinde Pollak (GDR)	22.9.1973

100 metres hurdles, shot, high jump, long jump, 800 metres

4765	Eva Wilms (Germany)	24.5.1977
4823	Eva Wilms (Germany)	18.6.1977
4839	Nadyezhda Tkachenko (USSR)	18.9.1977

Olympic Champions

Men

60 metres — sec.

1900	A. C. Kraenzlein (USA)	7·0
1904	A. Hahn (USA)	7·0

100 metres — sec.

1896	T. E. Burke (USA)	12·0
1900	F. W. Jarvis (USA)	11·0
1904	A. Hahn (USA)	11·0
1908	R. E. Walker (S. Africa)	10·8

100 metres – *contd*   sec.

1912	R. C. Craig (USA)	10·8
1920	C. W. Paddock (USA)	10·8
1924	H. M. Abrahams (GB)	10·6
1928	P. Williams (Canada)	10·8
1932	T. E. Tolan (USA)	10·3
1936	J. C. Owens (USA)	10·3
1948	W. H. Dillard (USA)	10·3
1952	L. J. Remigino (USA)	10·4
1956	B. J. Morrow (USA)	10·5
1960	A. Hary (Germany)	10·2
1964	R. L. Hayes (USA)	10·0
1968	J. R. Hines (USA)	9·95
1972	V. Borzov (USSR)	10·14
1976	H. Crawford (Trinidad)	10·06

200 metres   sec.

1900	J. W. B. Tewksbury (USA)	22·2
1904*	A. Hahn (USA)	21·6
1908	R. Kerr (Canada)	22·6
1912	R. C. Craig (USA)	21·7
1920	A. Woodring (USA)	22·0
1924	J. V. Scholz (USA)	21·6
1928	P. Williams (Canada)	21·8
1932	T. E. Tolan (USA)	21·2
1936	J. C. Owens (USA)	20·7
1948	M. E. Patton (USA)	21·1
1952	A. W. Stanfield (USA)	20·7
1956	B. J. Morrow (USA)	20·6
1960	L. Berruti (Italy)	20·5
1964	H. Carr (USA)	20·3
1968	T. C. Smith (USA)	19·83

* Straight course.

200 metres – *contd*   sec.
1972   V. Borzov (USSR)   20·00
1976   D. Quarrie (Jamaica)   20·23

400 metres   sec.
1896   T. E. Burke (USA)   54·2
1900   M. W. Long (USA)   49·4
1904   H. L. Hillman (USA)   49·2
1908*   W. Halswelle (GB)   50·0
1912   C. D. Reidpath (USA)   48·2
1920   B. G. D. Rudd (S. Africa)   49·6
1924   E. H. Liddell (GB)   47·6
1928   R. J. Barbuti (USA)   47·8
1932   W. A. Carr (USA)   46·2
1936   A. F. Williams (USA)   46·5
1948   A. S. Wint (Jamaica)   46·2
1952   V. G. Rhoden (Jamaica)   45·9
1956   C. L. Jenkins (USA)   46·7
1960   O. C. Davis (USA)   44·9
1964   M. D. Larrabee (USA)   45·1
1968   L. Evans (USA)   43·86
1972   V. Matthews (USA)   44·66
1976   A. Juantorena (Cuba)   44·26

* Walk-over.

800 metres   min. sec.
1896   E. H. Flack (Australia)   2 11·0
1900   A. E. Tysoe (GB)   2 01·2
1904   J. D. Lightbody (USA)   1 56·0
1908   M. W. Sheppard (USA)   1 52·8
1912   J. E. Meredith (USA)   1 51·9
1920   A. G. Hill (GB)   1 53·4
1924   D. G. A. Lowe (GB)   1 52·4

800 metres – *contd*   min. sec.

1928	D. G. A. Lowe (GB)	1 51·8
1932	T. Hampson (GB)	1 49·7
1936	J. Y. Woodruff (USA)	1 52·9
1948	M. G. Whitfield (USA)	1 49·2
1952	M. G. Whitfield (USA)	1 49·2
1956	T. W. Courtney (USA)	1 47·7
1960	P. G. Snell (New Zealand)	1 46·3
1964	P. G. Snell (New Zealand)	1 45·1
1968	R. Doubell (Australia)	1 44·3
1972	D. Wottle (USA)	1 45·9
1976	A. Juantorena (Cuba)	1 43·5

1,500 metres   min. sec.

1896	E. H. Flack (Australia)	4 33·2
1900	C. Bennett (GB)	4 06·2
1904	J. D. Lightbody (USA)	4 05·4
1908	M. W. Sheppard (USA)	4 03·4
1912	A. N. S. Jackson (GB)	3 56·8
1920	A. G. Hill (GB)	4 01·8
1924	P. J. Nurmi (Finland)	3 53·6
1928	H. E. Larva (Finland)	3 53·2
1932	L. Beccali (Italy)	3 51·2
1936	J. E. Lovelock (New Zealand)	3 47·8
1948	H. Eriksson (Sweden)	3 49·8
1952	J. Barthel (Luxembourg)	3 45·1
1956	R. M. Delany (Ireland)	3 41·2
1960	H. J. Elliott (Australia)	3 35·6
1964	P. G. Snell (New Zealand)	3 38·1
1968	K. Keino (Kenya)	3 34·9
1972	P. Vasala (Finland)	3 36·3
1976	J. Walker (New Zealand)	3 39·2

3,000 metres team   min. sec.
1912   USA (T. S. Berna, N. S. Taber,
              G. V. Bonhag)   8 44·6
1920   USA (H. H. Brown, A. A. Schardt,
              I. C. Dresser)   8 45·4
1924   Finland (P. J. Nurmi, V. J. Ritola,
              E. Katz)   8 32·0

3 miles team   min. sec.
1908   GB (J. E. Deakin, A. J. Robertson,
              W. Coales)   14 39·6

5,000 metres team   min. sec.
1900   GB (C. Bennett, J. T. Rimmer,
              A. E. Tysoe, S. J. Robinson,
              S. Rowley)   15 20·0

5,000 metres   min. sec.
1912   H. Kolehmainen (Finland)   14 36·6
1920   J. Guillemot (France)   14 55·6
1924   P. J. Nurmi (Finland)   14 31·2
1928   V. J. Ritola (Finland)   14 38·0
1932   L. A. Lehtinen (Finland)   14 30·0
1936   G. Hockert (Finland)   14 22·2
1948   G. E. G. Reiff (Belgium)   14 17·6
1952   E. Zatopek (Czechoslovakia)   14 06·6
1956   V. Kuts (USSR)   13 39·6
1960   M. G. Halberg (New Zealand)   13 43·4
1964   R. K. Schul (USA)   13 49·8
1968   M. Gammoudi (Tunisia)   14 05·0
1972   L. Viren (Finland)   13 26·4
1976   L. Viren (Finland)   13 24·8

4 miles team   min. sec.
1904   New York A.C., USA (A. L.
                Newton, G. Underwood,
                P. H. Pilgrim, H. Valentine,
                D. C. Munson)   21 17·8

5 miles   min. sec.
1908   E. R. Voigt (GB)   25 11·2

10,000 metres   min. sec.
1912   H. Kolehmainen (Finland)   31 20·8
1920   P. J. Nurmi (Finland)   31 45·8
1924   V. J. Ritola (Finland)   30 23·2
1928   P. J. Nurmi (Finland)   30 18·8
1932   J. Kusocinski (Poland)   30 11·4
1936   I. Salminen (Finland)   30 15·4
1948   E. Zatopek (Czechoslovakia)   29 59·6
1952   E. Zatopek (Czechoslovakia)   29 17·0
1956   V. Kuts (USSR)   28 45·6
1960   P. Bolotnikov (USSR)   28 32·2
1964   W. M. Mills (USA)   28 24·4
1968   N. Temu (Kenya)   29 27·4
1972   L. Viren (Finland)   27 38·4
1976   L. Viren (Finland)   27 40·4

Marathon   hr min. sec.
1896*   S. Louis (Greece)   2 58 50·0
1900*   M. Theato (France)   2 59 45·0
1904*   T. J. Hicks (USA)   3 28 53·0
1908†   J. J. Hayes (USA)   2 55 18·4
1912*   K. K. McArthur (S. Africa)   2 36 54·8

* Under standard distance of 26 miles 385 yd.
† D. Pietri (Italy), first in 2 hr 54 min. 46·4 sec., disqualified.

Marathon – *contd*   hr min. sec.

1920	H. Kolehmainen (Finland)	2 32 35·8
1924	A. O. Stenroos (Finland)	2 41 22·6
1928	El Ouafi (France)	2 32 57·0
1932	J. C. Zabala (Argentine)	2 31 36·0
1936	K. Son (Japan)	2 29 19·2
1948	D. Cabrera (Argentine)	2 34 51·6
1952	E. Zatopek (Czechoslovakia)	2 23 03·2
1956	A. Mimoun (France)	2 25 00·0
1960	Abebe Bikila (Ethiopia)	2 15 16·2
1964	Abebe Bikila (Ethiopia)	2 12 11·2
1968	M. Wolde (Ethiopia)	2 20 26·4
1972	F. Shorter (USA)	2 12 19·8
1976	W. Cierpinski (GDR)	2 09 55·0

2,500 metres steeplechase   min. sec.

| 1900 | G. W. Orton (USA) | 7 34·4 |
| 1904 | J. D. Lightbody (USA) | 7 39·6 |

3,000 metres steeplechase   min. sec.

1920	P. Hodge (GB)	10 00·4
1924	V. J. Ritola (Finland)	9 33·6
1928	T. A. Loukola (Finland)	9 21·8
1932*	V. Iso-Hollo (Finland)	10 33·4
1936	V. Iso-Hollo (Finland)	9 03·8
1948	T. Sjostrand (Sweden)	9 04·6
1952	H. Ashenfelter (USA)	8 45·4
1956	C. W. Brasher (GB)	8 41·2
1960	Z. Krzyszkowiak (Poland)	8 34·2
1964	G. Roelants (Belgium)	8 30·8
1968	A. Biwott (Kenya)	8 51·0

* 460 metres over distance.

3,000 metres steeplechase – *contd*   min. sec.

		min. sec.
1972	K. Keino (Kenya)	8 23·6
1976	A. Garderud (Sweden)	8 08·0

3,200 metres steeplechase

		min. sec.
1908	A. Russell (GB)	10 47·8

4,000 metres steeplechase

		min. sec.
1900	J. T. Rimmer (GB)	12 58·4

8,000 metres cross-country

1912	Sweden (H. Andersson, J. Eke, J. Ternstrom). Winner: H. Kolehmainen (Finland).
1920	Finland (P. J. Nurmi, winner; H. Liimatainen, T. Koskenniemi).

10,000 metres cross-country

1924	Finland (P. J. Nurmi, winner; V. J. Ritola, H. Liimatainen).

100 metres hurdles (3 ft 3 in.)

		sec.
1896	T. P. Curtis (USA)	17·6

110 metres hurdles (3 ft 6 in.)

		sec.
1900	A. C. Kraenzlein (USA)	15·4
1904	F. W. Schule (USA)	16·0
1908	F. C. Smithson (USA)	15·0
1912	F. W. Kelly (USA)	15·1
1920	E. J. Thomson (Canada)	14·8
1924	D. C. Kinsey (USA)	15·0

110 metres hurdles (3 ft 6 in.) – *contd*   sec.

1928	S. J. M. Atkinson (S. Africa)	14·8
1932	G. J. Saling (USA)	14·6
1936	F. G. Towns (USA)	14·2
1948	W. F. Porter (USA)	13·9
1952	W. H. Dillard (USA)	13·7
1956	L. Q. Calhoun (USA)	13·5
1960	L. Q. Calhoun (USA)	13·8
1964	H. W. Jones (USA)	13·6
1968	W. Davenport (USA)	13·33
1972	R. Milburn (USA)	13·24
1976	G. Drut (France)	13·30

200 metres hurdles (2 ft 6 in.)   sec.

| 1900 | A. C. Kraenzlein (USA) | 25·4 |
| 1904 | H. L. Hillman (USA) | 25·4 |

400 metres hurdles (2 ft 6 in.)   sec.

| 1904 | H. L. Hillman (USA) | 53·0 |

400 metres hurdles (3 ft 0 in.)   sec.

1900	J. W. B. Tewksbury (USA)	57·6
1908	C. J. Bacon (USA)	55·0
1920	F. F. Loomis (USA)	54·0
1924	F. M. Taylor (USA)	52·6
1928	Lord Burghley (GB)	53·4
1932	R. M. N. Tisdall (Ireland)	51·7
1936	G. F. Hardin (USA)	52·4
1948	L. V. Cochran (USA)	51·1
1952	C. H. Moore (USA)	50·8
1956	G. A. Davis (USA)	50·1
1960	G. A. Davis (USA)	49·3
1964	W. J. Cawley (USA)	49·6

400 metres hurdles (3 ft 0 in.) – *contd*   sec.

1968	D. P. Hemery (GB)	48·12
1972	J. Akii-Bua (Uganda)	47·82
1976	E. Moses (USA)	47·64

4 × 100 metres relay   sec.

1912	GB (D. H. Jacobs, H. M. Macintosh, V. H. A. d'Arcy, W. R. Applegarth)	42·4
1920	USA (C. W. Paddock, J. V. Scholz, L. C. Murchison, M. M. Kirksey)	42·2
1924	USA (F. Hussey, L. A. Clarke, L. C. Murchison, J. A. Leconey)	41·0
1928	USA (F. C. Wykoff, J. F. Quinn, C. E. Borah, H. A. Russell)	41·0
1932	USA (R. A. Kiesel, E. Toppino, H. M. Dyer, F. C. Wykoff)	40·0
1936	USA (J. C. Owens, R. H. Metcalfe, F. Draper, F. C. Wykoff)	39·8
1948	USA (H. N. Ewell, L. C. Wright, W. H. Dillard, M. E. Patton)	40·6
1952	USA (F. D. Smith, W. H. Dillard, L. J. Remigino, A. W. Stanfield)	40·1
1956	USA (I. J. Murchison, L. King, W. T. Baker, B. J. Morrow)	39·5
1960*	Germany (B. Cullmann, A. Hary, W. Mahlendorf, K. M. Lauer)	39·5
1964	USA (O. P. Drayton, G. H. Ashworth, R. V. Stebbins, R. L. Hayes)	39·0
1968	USA (C. Greene, M. Pender, R. R. Smith, J. R. Hines)	38·23
1972	USA (L. Black, R. Taylor, G. Tinker, E. Hart)	38·19

* USA (F. J. Budd, O. R. Norton, S. E. Johnson, D. W. Sime) first in 39·4 sec., disqualified.

4×100 metres relay – *contd*   sec.
1912   USA (H. Glance, J. Jones,
                M. Hampton, S. Riddick)   38·33

1,600 metres medley relay   min. sec.
1908   USA (W. F. Hamilton, N. J. Cartmell,
                J. B. Taylor, M. W. Sheppard)   3 29·4

4×400 metres relay   min. sec.
1912   USA (M. W. Sheppard,
                E. F. J. Lindberg, J. E. Meredith,
                C. D. Reidpath)   3 16·6
1920   GB (C. R. Griffiths, R. A. Lindsay,
                J. C. Ainsworth-Davis, G. M. Butler)   3 22·2
1924   USA (C. S. Cochrane, W. E. Stevenson,
                J. O. McDonald, A. B. Helffrich)   3 16·0
1928   USA (G. Baird, E. M. Spencer,
                E. P. Alderman, R. J. Barbuti)   3 14·2
1932   USA (I. Fuqua, E. A. Ablowich,
                K. D. Warner, W. A. Carr)   3 08·2
1936   GB (F. F. Wolff, G. L. Rampling,
                W. Roberts, A. G. K. Brown)   3 09·0
1948   USA (A. H. Harnden, C. F. Bourland,
                L. V. Cochran, M. G. Whitfield)   3 10·4
1952   Jamaica (A. S. Wint, L. A. Laing,
                H. H. McKenley, V. G. Rhoden)   3 03·9
1956   USA (C. L. Jenkins, L. W. Jones,
                J. W. Mashburn, T. W. Courtney)   3 04·8
1960   USA (J. L. Yerman, E. V. Young,
                G. A. Davis, O. C. Davis)   3 02·2
1964   USA (O. C. Cassell, M. D. Larrabee,
                U. C. Williams, H. Carr)   3 00·7
1968   USA (V. Matthews, R. Freeman,
                L. James, L. Evans)   2 56·1

4 × 400 metres relay – *contd*   min. sec.

| 1972 | Kenya (C. Asati, H. Nyamau, R. Ouko, J. Sang) | 2 59·8 |
| 1976 | USA (H. Frazier, B. Brown, F. Newhouse, M. Parks) | 2 58·7 |

High jump   metres

1896	E. H. Clark (USA)	1·81
1900	I. K. Baxter (USA)	1·90
1904	S. S. Jones (USA)	1·80
1908	H. F. Porter (USA)	1·90
1912	A. W. Richards (USA)	1·93
1920	R. W. Landon (USA)	1·94
1924	H. M. Osborn (USA)	1·98
1928	R. W. King (USA)	1·94
1932	D. McNaughton (Canada)	1·97
1936	C. C. Johnson (USA)	2·03
1948	J. A. Winter (Australia)	1·98
1952	W. F. Davis (USA)	2·04
1956	C. E. Dumas (USA)	2·12
1960	R. Shavlakadze (USSR)	2·16
1964	V. Brumel (USSR)	2·18
1968	R. Fosbury (USA)	2·24
1972	J. Tarmak (USSR)	2·23
1976	J. Wszola (Poland)	2·25

Standing high jump   metres

1900	R. C. Ewry (USA)	1·65
1904	R. C. Ewry (USA)	1·50
1908	R. C. Ewry (USA)	1·57
1912	P. Adams (USA)	1·63

Pole vault

		metres
1896	W. W. Hoyt (USA)	3·30
1900	I. K. Baxter (USA)	3·30
1904	C. E. Dvorak (USA)	3·50
1908	E. T. Cooke (USA) and A. C. Gilbert (USA)	3·71
1912	H. S. Babcock (USA)	3·95
1920	F. K. Foss (USA)	4·09
1924	L. S. Barnes (USA)	3·95
1928	S. W. Carr (USA)	4·20
1932	W. W. Miller (USA)	4·32
1936	E. E. Meadows (USA)	4·35
1948	O. G. Smith (USA)	4·30
1952	R. E. Richards (USA)	4·55
1956	R. E. Richards (USA)	4·56
1960	D. G. Bragg (USA)	4·70
1964	F. M. Hansen (USA)	5·10
1968	R. Seagren (USA)	5·40
1972	W. Nordwig (GDR)	5·50
1976	T. Slusarski (Poland)	5·50

Long jump

		metres
1896	E. H. Clark (USA)	6·35
1900	A. C. Kraenzlein (USA)	7·18
1904	M. Prinstein (USA)	7·34
1908	F. C. Irons (USA)	7·48
1912	A. L. Gutterson (USA)	7·60
1920	W. Pettersson (Sweden)*	7·15
1924	W. De H. Hubbard (USA)	7·44
1928	E. B. Hamm (USA)	7·73
1932	E. L. Gordon (USA)	7·64
1936	J. C. Owens (USA)	8·06
1948	W. S. Steele (USA)	7·82

* Later known as Bjorneman.

Long jump – *contd*   metres
1952   J. C. Biffle (USA)   7·57
1956   G. C. Bell (USA)   7·83
1960   R. H. Boston (USA)   8·12
1964   L. Davies (GB)   8·07
1968   R. Beamon (USA)   8·90
1972   R. Williams (USA)   8·24
1976   A. Robinson (USA)   8·35

Standing long jump   metres
1900   R. C. Ewry (USA)   3·21
1904   R. C. Ewry (USA)   3·46
1908   R. C. Ewry (USA)   3·33
1912   C. Tsciclitiras (Greece)   3·37

Triple jump   metres
1896*   J. V. Connolly (USA)   13·71
1900   M. Prinstein (USA)   14·47
1904   M. Prinstein (USA)   14·35
1908   T. J. Ahearne (GB/Ire)   14·91
1912   G. Lindblom (Sweden)   14·76
1920   V. Tuulos (Finland)   14·50
1924   A. W. Winter (Australia)   15·52
1928   M. Oda (Japan)   15·21
1932   C. Nambu (Japan)   15·72
1936   N. Tajima (Japan)   16·00
1948   A. P. Ahman (Sweden)   15·40
1952   A. F. da Silva (Brazil)   16·22
1956   A. F. da Silva (Brazil)   16·35
1960   J. Szmidt (Poland)   16·81
1964   J. Szmidt (Poland)   16·85
1968   V. Saneyev (USSR)   17·39

* Two hops and one jump.

Triple jump – *contd*		metres
1972	V. Saneyev (USSR)	17·35
1976	V. Saneyev (USSR)	17·29

Standing triple jump		metres
1900	R. C. Ewry (USA)	10·57
1904	R. C. Ewry (USA)	10·54

Shot		metres
1896*	R. S. Garrett (USA)	11·22
1900*	R. Sheldon (USA)	14·10
1904	R. W. Rose (USA)	14·81
1908	R. W. Rose (USA)	14·21
1912	P. J. McDonald (USA)	15·34
1920	V. Porhola (Finland)	14·81
1924	C. L. Houser (USA)	14·99
1928	J. Kuck (USA)	15·87
1932	L. J. Sexton (USA)	16·01
1936	H. Woellke (Germany)	16·20
1948	W. M. Thompson (USA)	17·12
1952	W. P. O'Brien (USA)	17·41
1956	W. P. O'Brien (USA)	18·57
1960	W. H. Nieder (USA)	19·68
1964	D. C. Long (USA)	20·33
1968	J. R. Matson (USA)	20·54
1972	W. Komar (Poland)	21·18
1976	U. Beyer (GDR)	21·05

* From 7 ft square.

Shot (both hands)		metres
1912	R. W. Rose (USA)	27·69

Discus		metres
1896	R. S. Garrett (USA)	29·14
1900	R. Bauer (Hungary)	36·04

Discus – *contd*   metres

1904	M. J. Sheridan (USA)	39·28
1908	M. J. Sheridan (USA)	40·88
1912	A. R. Taipale (Finland)	45·20
1920	E. Niklander (Finland)	44·68
1924	C. L. Houser (USA)	46·16
1928	C. L. Houser (USA)	47·32
1932	J. F. Anderson (USA)	49·48
1936	K. K. Carpenter (USA)	50·48
1948	A. Consolini (Italy)	52·78
1952	S. G. Iness (USA)	55·02
1956	A. A. Oerter (USA)	56·36
1960	A. A. Oerter (USA)	59·18
1964	A. A. Oerter (USA)	61·00
1968	A. A. Oerter (USA)	64·78
1972	L. Danek (Czechoslovakia)	64·40
1976	M. Wilkins (USA)	67·50

Discus (Greek style)   metres

1908	M. J. Sheridan (USA)	38·00

Discus (both hands)   metres

1912	A. R. Taipale (Finland)	82·86

Hammer   metres

1900*	J. J. Flanagan (USA)	49·72
1904	J. J. Flanagan (USA)	51·22
1908	J. J. Flanagan (USA)	51·92
1912	M. J. McGrath (USA)	54·74
1920	P. J. Ryan (USA)	52·88
1924	F. D. Tootell (USA)	53·30
1928	P. O'Callaghan (Ireland)	51·38

* From 9 ft circle.

Hammer – *contd*   metres
1932   P. O'Callaghan (Ireland)   53·92
1936   K. Hein (Germany)   56·48
1948   I. Nemeth (Hungary)   56·06
1952   J. Csermak (Hungary)   60·34
1956   H. V. Connolly (USA)   63·18
1960   V. Rudenkov (USSR)   67·10
1964   R. Klim (USSR)   69·74
1968   G. Zsivotzky (Hungary)   73·36
1972   A. Bondarchuk (USSR)   75·50
1976   Y. Sedykh (USSR)   77·52

Javelin   metres
1908   E. V. Lemming (Sweden)   54·82
1912   E. V. Lemming (Sweden)   60·64
1920   J. J. Myyra (Finland)   65·78
1924   J. J. Myyra (Finland)   62·96
1928   E. H. Lundkvist (Sweden)   66·60
1932   M. H. Jarvinen (Finland)   72·70
1936   G. Stock (Germany)   71·84
1948   K. T. Rautavaara (Finland)   69·76
1952   C. C. Young (USA)   73·78
1956   E. Danielsen (Norway)   85·70
1960   V. Tsibulenko (USSR)   84·64
1964   P. L. Nevala (Finland)   82·66
1968   J. Lusis (USSR)   90·10
1972   K. Wolfermann (Germany)   90·48
1976   M. Nemeth (Hungary)   94·58

Javelin (free style)   metres
1908   E. V. Lemming (Sweden)   54·44

Javelin (both hands)   metres
1912   J. Saaristo (Finland)   109·40

56 lb weight   metres
1904   E. Desmartreau (Canada)   10·46
1920   P. McDonald (USA)   11·28

Pentathlon
1912*   F. Bie (Norway)
1920   E. Lehtonen (Finland)
1924   E. Lehtonen (Finland)

* J. H. Thorpe (USA), first, subsequently debarred.

Decathlon (1962 Tables)   pts
1912*   H. Wieslander (Sweden)   6161
1920   H. Lovland (Norway)   5970
1924   H. M. Osborn (USA)   6668
1928   P. I. Yrjola (Finland)   6774
1932   J. A. B. Bausch (USA)   6896
1936   G. E. Morris (USA)   7421
1948   R. B. Mathias (USA)   6825
1952   R. B. Mathias (USA)   7731
1956   M. G. Campbell (USA)   7708
1960   R. L. Johnson (USA)   8001
1964   W. Holdorf (Germany)   7887
1968   W. Toomey (USA)   8193
1972   N. Avilov (USSR)   8454
1976   B. Jenner (USA)   8618

* J. H. Thorpe (USA), first with 6756, subsequently debarred.

3,000 metres walk   min. sec.
1920   U. Frigerio (Italy)   13 14·2

150

3,500 metres walk

		min.	sec.
1908	G. E. Larner (GB)	14	55·0

10,000 metres walk

		min.	sec.
1912	G. H. Goulding (Canada)	46	28·4
1920	U. Frigerio (Italy)	48	06·2
1924	U. Frigerio (Italy)	47	49·0
1948	J. F. Mikaelsson (Sweden)	45	13·2
1952	J. F. Mikaelsson (Sweden)	45	02·8

10 mile walk

		hr	min.	sec.
1908	G. E. Larner (GB)	1	15	57·4

20,000 metres walk

		hr	min.	sec.
1956	L. Spirin (USSR)	1	31	27·4
1960	V. Golubnichiy (USSR)	1	34	07·2
1964	K. J. Matthews (GB)	1	29	34·0
1968	V. Golubnichiy (USSR)	1	33	58·4
1972	P. Frenkel (GDR)	1	26	42·4
1976	D. Bautista (Mexico)	1	24	40·6

50,000 metres walk

		hr	min.	sec.
1932	T. W. Green (GB)	4	50	10·0
1936	H. H. Whitlock (GB)	4	30	41·4
1948	J. A. Ljunggren (Sweden)	4	41	52·0
1952	G. Dordoni (Italy)	4	28	07·8
1956	N. R. Read (New Zealand)	4	30	42·8
1960	D. J. Thompson (GB)	4	25	30·0
1964	A. Pamich (Italy)	4	11	12·4
1968	C. Hohne (GDR)	4	20	13·6
1972	B. Kannenberg (Germany)	3	56	11·6
1976	Not held			

Women

100 metres

		sec.
1928	E. Robinson (USA)	12·2
1932	S. Walasiewicz (Poland)	11·9
1936	H. H. Stephens (USA)	11·5
1948	F. E. Blankers-Koen (Netherlands)	11·9
1952	M. Jackson (Australia)	11·5
1956	B. Cuthbert (Australia)	11·5
1960	W. G. Rudolph (USA)	11·0
1964	W. Tyus (USA)	11·4
1968	W. Tyus (USA)	11·07
1972	R. Stecher (GDR)	11·07
1976	A. Richter (Germany)	11·08

200 metres

		sec.
1948	F. E. Blankers-Koen (Netherlands)	24·4
1952	M. Jackson (Australia)	23·7
1956	B. Cuthbert (Australia)	23·4
1960	W. G. Rudolph (USA)	24·0
1964	E. M. McGuire (USA)	23·0
1968	I. Szewinska (Poland)	22·58
1972	R. Stecher (GDR)	22·40
1976	B. Eckert (GDR)	22·37

400 metres

		sec.
1964	B. Cuthbert (Australia)	52·0
1968	C. Besson (France)	52·03
1972	M. Zehrt (GDR)	51·08
1976	I. Szewinska (Poland)	49·29

800 metres   min. sec.
1928   L. Radke (Germany)   2 16·8
1960   L. Lysenko (USSR)   2 04·3
1964   A. E. Packer (GB)   2 01·1
1968   M. Manning (USA)   2 00·9
1972   H. Falck (Germany)   1 58·6
1976   T. Kazankina (USSR)   1 54·9

1,500 metres   min. sec.
1972   L. Bragina (USSR)   4 01·4
1976   T. Kazankina (USSR)   4 05·5

80 metres hurdles   sec.
1932   M. Didrikson (USA)   11·7
1936   T. Valla (Italy)   11·7
1948   F. E. Blankers-Koen (Netherlands)   11·2
1952   S. B. De La Hunty (Australia)   10·9
1956   S. B. De La Hunty (Australia)   10·7
1960   I. Press (USSR)   10·8
1964   K. Balzer (Germany)   10·5
1968   M. Caird (Australia)   10·3

100 metres hurdles   sec.
1972   A. Ehrhardt (GDR)   12·59
1976   J. Schaller (GDR)   12·77

4 × 100 metres relay   sec.
1928   Canada (F. Rosenfeld, F. Bell,
              E. Smith, M. Cook)   48·4
1932   USA (M. L. Carew, E. Furtsch,
              A. J. Rogers, W. von Bremen)   47·0
1936   USA (H. C. Bland, A. J. Rogers,
              E. Robinson, H. H. Stephens)   46·9

4 × 100 metres relay – *contd*   sec.

1948	Netherlands (X. Stad-de-Jongh, J. M. Witziers, G. J. M. Koudijs, F. E. Blankers-Koen)	47·5
1952	USA (M. E. Faggs, B. P. Jones, J. T. Moreau, C. Hardy)	45·9
1956	Australia (S. B. De La Hunty, N. W. Croker, F. N. Mellor, B. Cuthbert)	44·5
1960	USA (M. Hudson, L. Williams, B. P. Jones, W. G. Rudolph)	44·5
1964	Poland (T. B. Ciepla, I. Szewinska, H. Gorecka, E. Klobukowska)	43·6
1968	USA (B. Ferrell, M. Bailes, M. Netter, W. Tyus)	42·87
1972	Germany (C. Krause, I. Mickler, A. Richter, H. Rosendahl)	42·81
1976	GDR (M. Oelsner, R. Stecher, C. Bodendorf, B. Eckert)	42·55

4 × 400 metres relay   min. sec.

1972	GDR (D. Kasling, R. Kuhne, H. Seidler, M. Zehrt)	3 23·0
1976	GDR (D. Maletzki, B. Rohde, E. Streidt, C. Brehmer)	3 19·2

High jump   metres

1928	E. Catherwood (Canada)	1·59
1932	J. H. Shiley (USA)	1·65
1936	I. Csak (Hungary)	1·60
1948	A. Coachman (USA)	1·68
1952	E. C. Brand (S. Africa)	1·67
1956	M. I. McDaniel (USA)	1·76
1960	I. Balas (Romania)	1·85
1964	I. Balas (Romania)	1·90

High jump – *contd*   metres
1968   M. Rezkova (Czechoslovakia)   1·82
1972   U. Meyfarth (Germany)   1·92
1976   R. Ackermann (GDR)   1·93

Long jump   metres
1948   V. O. Gyarmati (Hungary)   5·70
1952   Y. W. Williams (New Zealand)   6·24
1956   E. Krzesinska (Poland)   6·35
1960   V. Krepkina (USSR)   6·37
1964   M. D. Rand (GB)   6·76
1968   V. Viscopoleanu (Romania)   6·82
1972   H. Rosendahl (Germany)   6·78
1976   A. Voigt (GDR)   6·72

Shot   metres
1948   M. O. M. Ostermeyer (France)   13·75
1952   G. I. Zybina (USSR)   15·28
1956   T. A. Tyshkevich (USSR)   16·59
1960   T. Press (USSR)   17·32
1964   T. Press (USSR)   18·14
1968   M. Gummel (GDR)   19·61
1972   N. Chizhova (USSR)   21·03
1976   I. Khristova (Bulgaria)   21·16

Discus   metres
1928   H. Konopacka (Poland)   39·62
1932   L. Copeland (USA)   40·58
1936   G. Mauermayer (Germany)   47·62
1948   M. O. M. Ostermeyer (France)   41·92
1952   N. Romashkova (USSR)   51·42
1956   O. Fikotova (Czechoslovakia)   53·68
1960   N. Ponomaryeva, *née* Romashkova
             (USSR)   55·10

Discus – *contd*   metres
1964   T. Press (USSR)   57·26
1968   L. Manoliu (Romania)   58·28
1972   F. Melnik (USSR)   66·62
1976   E. Schlaak (GDR)   69·00

Javelin   metres
1932   M. Didrikson (USA)   43·68
1936   T. Fleischer (Germany)   45·18
1948   H. Bauma (Austria)   45·56
1952   D. Zatopkova (Czechoslovakia)   50·46
1956   I. Jaunzeme (USSR)   53·86
1960   E. Ozolina (USSR)   55·98
1964   M. Penes (Romania)   60·54
1968   A. Nemeth (Hungary)   60·36
1972   R. Fuchs (GDR)   63·88
1976   R. Fuchs (GDR)   65·94

Pentathlon   pts
1964   I. Press (USSR)   5246
1968   I. Becker (Germany)   5098
1972*   M. E. Peters (GB)   4801
1976*   S. Siegl (GDR)   4745

* Scored on 1970 Tables.

European Champions

Men

100 metres   sec.
1934   C. D. Berger (Netherlands)   10·5

100 metres – *contd*

		sec.
1938	M. B. Osendarp (Netherlands)	10·5
1946	J. Archer (GB)	10·6
1950	E. Bally (France)	10·7
1954	H. Futterer (Germany)	10·5
1958	A. Hary (Germany)	10·3
1962	C. Piquemal (France)	10·4
1966	W. J. Maniak (Poland)	10·5
1969	V. Borzov (USSR)	10·4
1971	V. Borzov (USSR)	10·3
1974	V. Borzov (USSR)	10·27
1978	P. Mennea (Italy)	10·27

200 metres

		sec.
1934	C. D. Berger (Netherlands)	21·5
1938	M. B. Osendarp (Netherlands)	21·2
1946	N. Karakulov (USSR)	21·6
1950	B. Shenton (GB)	21·5
1954	H. Futterer (Germany)	20·9
1958	M. Germar (Germany)	21·0
1962	O. Jonsson (Sweden)	20·7
1966	R. Bambuck (France)	20·9
1969	P. Clerc (Switzerland)	20·6
1971	V. Borzov (USSR)	20·3
1974	P. Mennea (Italy)	20·60
1978	P. Mennea (Italy)	20·16

400 metres

		sec.
1934	A. Metzner (Germany)	47·9
1938	A. G. K. Brown (GB)	47·4
1946	N. Holst Sorensen (Denmark)	47·9
1950	D. C. Pugh (GB)	47·3
1954	A. Ignatyev (USSR)	46·6
1958	J. D. Wrighton (GB)	46·3

400 metres – *contd*   sec.
1962	R. I. Brightwell (GB)	45·9
1966	S. Gredzinski (Poland)	46·0
1969	J. Werner (Poland)	45·7
1971	D. A. Jenkins (GB)	45·5
1974	K. Honz (Germany)	45·04
1978	F-P. Hofmeister (Germany)	45·73

800 metres   min. sec.
1934	M. Szabo (Hungary)	1	52·0
1938	R. Harbig (Germany)	1	50·6
1946	R. Gustafsson (Sweden)	1	51·0
1950	H. J. Parlett (GB)	1	50·5
1954	L. Szentgali (Hungary)	1	47·1
1958	M. A. Rawson (GB)	1	47·8
1962	M. Matuschewski (GDR)	1	50·5
1966	M. Matuschewski (GDR)	1	45·9
1969	D. Fromm (GDR)	1	45·9
1971	Y. Arzhanov (USSR)	1	45·6
1974	L. Susanj (Yugoslavia)	1	44·1
1978	O. Beyer (GDR)	1	43·8

1,500 metres   min. sec.
1934	L. Beccali (Italy)	3	54·6
1938	S. C. Wooderson (GB)	3	53·6
1946	L. Strand (Sweden)	3	48·0
1950	W. F. Slijkhuis (Netherlands)	3	47·2
1954	R. G. Bannister (GB)	3	43·8
1958	B. S. Hewson (GB)	3	41·9
1962	M. Jazy (France)	3	40·9
1966	B. Tummler (Germany)	3	41·9
1969	J. H. Whetton (GB)	3	39·4
1971	F. Arese (Italy)	3	38·4

1,500 metres – *contd*   min. sec.
1974   K. P. Justus (GDR)   3 40·6
1978   S. Ovett (GB)   3 35·6

5,000 metres   min. sec.
1934   R. Rochard (France)   14 36·8
1938   T. A. Maki (Finland)   14 26·8
1946   S. C. Wooderson (GB)   14 08·6
1950   E. Zatopek (Czechoslovakia)   14 03·0
1954   V. Kuts (USSR)   13 56·6
1958   Z. Krzyszkowiak (Poland)   13 53·4
1962   M. B. S. Tulloh (GB)   14 00·6
1966   M. Jazy (France)   13 42·8
1969   I. Stewart (GB)   13 44·8
1971   J. Vaatainen (Finland)   13 32·6
1974   B. Foster (GB)   13 17·2
1978   V. Ortis (Italy)   13 28·5

10,000 metres   min. sec.
1934   I. Salminen (Finland)   31 02·6
1938   I. Salminen (Finland)   30 52·4
1946   V. J. Heino (Finland)   29 52·0
1950   E. Zatopek (Czechoslovakia)   29 12·0
1954   E. Zatopek (Czechoslovakia)   28 58·0
1958   Z. Krzyszkowiak (Poland)   28 56·0
1962   P. Bolotnikov (USSR)   28 54·0
1966   J. Haase (GDR)   28 26·0
1969   J. Haase (GDR)   28 41·6
1971   J. Vaatainen (Finland)   27 52·8
1974   M. Kuschmann (GDR)   28 25·8
1978   M. Vainio (Finland)   27 31·0

Marathon

		hr min. sec.
1934	A. A. Toivonen (Finland)	2 52 29·0
1938	V. Muinonen (Finland)	2 37 28·8
1946*	M. Hietanen (Finland)	2 24 55·0
1950	J. T. Holden (GB)	2 32 13·2
1954	V. L. Karvonen (Finland)	2 24 51·5
1958	S. Popov (USSR)	2 15 17·0
1962	B. L. Kilby (GB)	2 23 18·8
1966	J. J. Hogan (GB)	2 20 04·6
1969	R. Hill (GB)	2 16 47·8
1971	K. Lismont (Belgium)	2 13 09·0
1974	I. R. Thompson (GB)	2 13 18·8
1978	L. Moseyev (USSR)	2 11 57·5

* Under standard distance of 26 miles 385 yd.

3,000 metres steeplechase

		min. sec.
1938	L. A. Larsson (Sweden)	9 16·2
1946	R. Pujazon (France)	9 01·4
1950	J. Roudny (Czechoslovakia)	9 05·4
1954	S. Rozsnyoi (Hungary)	8 49·6
1958	J. Chromik (Poland)	8 38·2
1962	G. Roelants (Belgium)	8 32·6
1966	V. Kudinskiy (USSR)	8 26·6
1969	M. Zhelev (Bulgaria)	8 25·0
1971	J-P. Villain (France)	8 25·2
1974	B. Malinowski (Poland)	8 15·0
1978	B. Malinowski (Poland)	8 15·1

110 metres hurdles

		sec.
1934	J. Kovacs (Hungary)	14·8
1938	D. O. Finlay (GB)	14·3
1946	E. H. Lidman (Sweden)	14·6
1950	A. J. Marie (France)	14·6

110 metres hurdles – *contd*   sec.

1954	Y. Bulanchik (USSR)	14·4
1958	K. M. Lauer (Germany)	13·7
1962	A. Mikhailov (USSR)	13·8
1966	E. Ottoz (Italy)	13·7
1969	E. Ottoz (Italy)	13·5
1971	F. Siebeck (GDR)	14·0
1974	G. Drut (France)	13·40
1978	T. Munkelt (GDR)	13·54

400 metres hurdles   sec.

1934	H. Scheele (Germany)	53·2
1938	P. Joye (France)	53·1
1946	B. Storskrubb (Finland)	52·2
1950	A. Filiput (Italy)	51·9
1954	A. Yulin (USSR)	50·5
1958	Y. Lituyev (USSR)	51·1
1962	S. Morale (Italy)	49·2
1966	R. Frinolli (Italy)	49·8
1969	V. Skomorokhov (USSR)	49·7
1971	J-C Nallet (France)	49·2
1974	A. P. Pascoe (GB)	48·82
1978	H. Schmid (Germany)	48·51

4 × 100 metres relay   sec.

1934	Germany (E. Schein, E. Gillmeister, G. Hornberger, E. Borchmeyer)	41·0
1938	Germany (M. Kersch, G. Hornberger, K. Neckermann, J. Scheuring)	40·9
1946	Sweden (S. Danielsson, I. Nilsson, O. Laessker, S. Hakansson)	41·5
1950	USSR (V. Sukharyev, L. Kalyayev, L. Sanadze, N. Karakulov)	41·5

4 × 100 metres relay – *contd*
sec.

1954	Hungary (L. Zarandi, G. Varasdi, G. Csanyi, B. Goldovanyi)	40·6
1958	Germany (W. Mahlendorf, A. Hary, H. Futterer, M. Germar)	40·2
1962	Germany (K. Ulonska, P. Gamper, H. J. Bender, M. Germar)	39·5
1966	France (M. Berger, J. Delecour, C. Piquemal, R. Bambuck)	39·4
1969	France (A. Sarteur, P. Bourbeillon, G. Fenouil, F. Saint-Gilles)	38·8
1971	Czechoslovakia (L. Kriz, J. Demec, J. Kynos, L. Bohman)	39·3
1974	France (L. Sainte-Rose, J. Arame, B. Cherrier, D. Chauvelot)	38·69
1978	Poland (Z. Nowosz, Z. Licznerski, L. Dunecki, M. Woronin)	38·58

4 × 400 metres relay
min. sec.

1934	Germany (H. Hamann, H. Scheele, H. Voigt, A. Metzner)	3 14·1
1938	Germany (H. Blazejezak, M. Bues, E. Linnhoff, R. Harbig)	3 13·7
1946	France (B. Santona, Y. Cros, R. Chefd'hotel, J. Lunis)	3 14·4
1950	GB (M. W. Pike, L. C. Lewis, A. W. Scott, D. C. Pugh)	3 10·2
1954*	France (P. Haarhoff, J. Degats, J. P. Martin du Gard, J. P. Goudeau)	3 08·7
1958	GB (E. J. Sampson, J. MacIsaac, J. D. Wrighton, J. E. Salisbury)	3 07·9

* GB (F. P. Higgins, A. Dick, P. G. Fryer, D. J. N. Johnson), first in 3 min. 08·2 sec., disqualified.

4 × 400 metres relay – *contd*   min. sec.

1962	Germany (M. Kinder, W. Kindermann, H. J. Reske, J. Schmitt)	3 05·8
1966	Poland (J. Werner, E. Borowski, S. Gredzinski, A. Badenski)	3 04·5
1969	France (G. Bertould, C. Nicolau, J. Carette, J-C. Nallet)	3 02·3
1971	Germany (H-R. Schloske, T. Jordan, M. Jellinghaus, H. Kohler)	3 02·9
1974	GB (G. H. Cohen, W. J. Hartley, A. P. Pascoe, D. A. Jenkins)	3 03·3
1978	Germany (M. Weppler, F-P. Hofmeister, B. Herrmann, H. Schmid)	3 02·0

High jump   metres

1934	K. Kotkas (Finland)	2·00
1938	K. Lundqvist (Sweden)	1·97
1946	A. Bolinder (Sweden)	1·99
1950	A. S. Paterson (GB)	1·96
1954	B. Nilsson (Sweden)	2·02
1958	R. Dahl (Sweden)	2·12
1962	V. Brumel (USSR)	2·21
1966	J. Madubost (France)	2·12
1969	V. Gavrilov (USSR)	2·17
1971	K. Sapka (USSR)	2·20
1974	J. Torring (Denmark)	2·25
1978	V. Yashchenko (USSR)	2·30

Pole vault   metres

1934	G. Wegner (Germany)	4·00
1938	K. Sutter (Germany)	4·05
1946	A. Lindberg (Sweden)	4·17
1950	R. L. Lundberg (Sweden)	4·30

Pole vault – *contd*

		metres
1954	E. Landstrom (Finland)	4·40
1958	E. Landstrom (Finland)	4·50
1962	P. Nikula (Finland)	4·80
1966	W. Nordwig (GDR)	5·10
1969	W. Nordwig (GDR)	5·30
1971	W. Nordwig (GDR)	5·35
1974	V. Kishkun (USSR)	5·35
1978	V. Trofimenko (USSR)	5·55

Long jump

		metres
1934	W. Leichum (Germany)	7·45
1938	W. Leichum (Germany)	7·64
1946	O. Laessker (Sweden)	7·42
1950	T. Bryngeirsson (Iceland)	7·32
1954	O. Foldessy (Hungary)	7·51
1958	I. Ter-Ovanesyan (USSR)	7·81
1962	I. Ter-Ovanesyan (USSR)	8·19
1966	L. Davies (GB)	7·98
1969	I. Ter-Ovanesyan (USSR)	8·17
1971	M. Klauss (GDR)	7·92
1974	V. Podluzhny (USSR)	8·12
1978	J. Rousseau (France)	8·18

Triple jump

		metres
1934	W. Peters (Netherlands)	14·89
1938	O. Rajasaari (Finland)	15·32
1946	K. J. V. Rautio (Finland)	15·17
1950	L. Shcherbakov (USSR)	15·39
1954	L. Shcherbakov (USSR)	15·90
1958	J. Szmidt (Poland)	16·43
1962	J. Szmidt (Poland)	16·55
1966	G. Stoikovski (Bulgaria)	16·67
1969	V. Sanyeyev (USSR)	17·34

Triple jump – *contd*   metres
1971	J. Drehmel (GDR)	17·16
1974	V. Sanyeyev (USSR)	17·23
1978	M. Srejovic (Yugoslavia)	16·94

Shot   metres
1934	A. Viiding (Estonia)	15·19
1938	A. Kreek (Estonia)	15·83
1946	G. Huseby (Iceland)	15·56
1950	G. Huseby (Iceland)	16·74
1954	J. Skobla (Czechoslovakia)	17·20
1958	A. Rowe (GB)	17·78
1962	V. Varju (Hungary)	19·02
1966	V. Varju (Hungary)	19·43
1969	D. Hoffmann (GDR)	20·12
1971	H. Briesenick (GDR)	21·08
1974	H. Briesenick (GDR)	20·50
1978	U. Beyer (GDR)	21·08

Discus   metres
1934	H. Andersson (Sweden)	50·38
1938	W. Schroeder (Germany)	49·70
1946	A. Consolini (Italy)	53·22
1950	A. Consolini (Italy)	53·74
1954	A. Consolini (Italy)	53·44
1958	E. Piatkowski (Poland)	53·92
1962	V. Trusenyov (USSR)	57·10
1966	D. Thorith (GDR)	57·42
1969	H. Losch (GDR)	61·82
1971	L. Danek (Czechoslovakia)	63·90
1974	P. Kahma (Finland)	63·62
1978	W. Schmidt (GDR)	66·82

Hammer

		metres
1934	V. Porhola (Finland)	50·34
1938	K. Hein (Germany)	58·76
1946	B. Ericson (Sweden)	56·44
1950	S. Strandli (Norway)	55·70
1954	M. Krivonosov (USSR)	63·34
1958	T. Rut (Poland)	64·78
1962	G. Zsivotsky (Hungary)	69·64
1966	R. Klim (USSR)	70·02
1969	A. Bondarchuk (USSR)	74·68
1971	U. Beyer (Germany)	72·36
1974	A. Spiridonov (USSR)	74·20
1978	Y. Sedykh (USSR)	77·28

Javelin

		metres
1934	M. H. Jarvinen (Finland)	76·66
1938	M. H. Jarvinen (Finland)	76·86
1946	A. L. F. Atterwall (Sweden)	68·74
1950	T. Hyytiainen (Finland)	71·26
1954	J. Sidlo (Poland)	76·34
1958	J. Sidlo (Poland)	80·18
1962	J. Lusis (USSR)	82·04
1966	J. Lusis (USSR)	84·48
1969	J. Lusis (USSR)	91·52
1971	J. Lusis (USSR)	90·68
1974	H. Siitonen (Finland)	89·58
1978	M. Wessing (Germany)	89·12

Decathlon (1962 Tables)

		pts
1934	H. H. Sievert (Germany)	6858
1938	O. Bexell (Sweden)	6870
1946	G. Holmvang (Norway)	6760
1950	I. Heinrich (France)	7009

Decathlon (1962 Tables) – *contd*   pts

1954	V. Kuznyetsov (USSR)	7043
1958	V. Kuznyetsov (USSR)	7697
1962	V. Kuznyetsov (USSR)	7770
1966	W. von Moltke (Germany)	7740
1969	J. Kirst (GDR)	8041
1971	J. Kirst (GDR)	8196
1974	R. Skowronek (Poland)	8207
1978	A. Grebenyuk (USSR)	8340

10,000 metres walk   min. sec.

1946	J. F. Mikaelsson (Sweden)	46 05·2
1950	F. Schwab (Switzerland)	46 01·8
1954	J. Dolezal (Czechoslovakia)	45 01·8

20,000 metres walk   hr min. sec.

1958	S. F. Vickers (GB)	1 33 09·0
1962	K. J. Matthews (GB)	1 35 54·8
1966	D. Lindner (GDR)	1 29 25·0
1969	V. P. Nihill (GB)	1 30 41·0
1971	N. Smaga (USSR)	1 27 20·2
1974	V. Golubnichiy (USSR)	1 29 30·0
1978	R. Wieser (GDR)	1 23 11·5

50,000 metres walk   hr min. sec.

1934	J. Dalins (Latvia)	4 49 52·6
1938	H. H. Whitlock (GB)	4 41 51·0
1946	J. Ljunggren (Sweden)	4 38 20·0
1950	G. Dordoni (Italy)	4 40 42·6
1954	V. Ukhov (USSR)	4 22 11·2
1958	Y. Maskinskov (USSR)	4 17 15·4
1962	A. Pamich (Italy)	4 18 46·6

50,000 metres walk – *contd*   hr min. sec.

1966	A. Pamich (Italy)	4	18	42·2
1969	C. Hohne (GDR)	4	13	32·0
1971	V. Soldatenko (USSR)	4	02	22·0
1974	C. Hohne (GDR)	3	59	05·6
1978	J. Llopart (Spain)	3	53	29·9

Women

100 metres   sec.

1938	S. Walasiewicz (Poland)	11·9
1946	Y. Sechenova (USSR)	11·9
1950	F. E. Blankers-Koen (Netherlands)	11·7
1954	I. Turova (USSR)	11·8
1958	H. J. Young (GB)	11·7
1962	D. Hyman (GB)	11·3
1966	E. Klobukowska (Poland)	11·5
1969	P. Vogt (GDR)	11·6
1971	R. Stecher (GDR)	11·4
1974	I. Szewinska (Poland)	11·13
1978	M. Gohr (GDR)	11·13

200 metres   sec.

1938	S. Walasiewicz (Poland)	23·8
1946	Y. Sechenova (USSR)	25·4
1950	F. E. Blankers-Koen (Netherlands)	24·0
1954	M. Itkina (USSR)	24·3
1958	B. Janiszewska (Poland)	24·1
1962	J. Heine (Germany)	23·5
1966	I. Kirszenstein (Poland)	23·1
1969	P. Vogt (GDR)	23·2
1971	R. Stecher (GDR)	22·7

200 metres – *contd*   sec.
1974   I. Szewinska* (Poland)   22·51
1978   L. Kondratyeva (USSR)   22·52

                    * *née* Kirszenstein.

400 metres   sec.
1958   M. Itkina (USSR)   53·7
1962   M. Itkina (USSR)   53·4
1966   A. Chmelkova (Czechoslovakia)   52·9
1969   N. Duclos (France)   51·7
1971   H. Seidler (GDR)   52·1
1974   R. Salin (Finland)   50·14
1978   M. Koch (GDR)   48·94

800 metres   min. sec.
1954   N. Otkalenko (USSR)   2 08·8
1958   Y. Yermolayeva (USSR)   2 06·3
1962   G. Kraan (Netherlands)   2 02·8
1966   V. Nikolic (Yugoslavia)   2 02·8
1969   L. B. Board (GB)   2 01·4
1971   V. Nikolic (Yugoslavia)   2 00·0
1974   L. Tomova (Bulgaria)   1 58·1
1978   T. Providokhina (USSR)   1 55·8

1,500 metres   min. sec.
1969   J. Jehlickova (Czechoslovakia)   4 10·7
1971   K. Burneleit (GDR)   4 09·6
1974   G. Hoffmeister (GDR)   4 02·3
1978   G. Romanova (USSR)   3 59·0

3,000 metres   min. sec.
1974   N. Holmen (Finland)   8 55·2
1978   S. Ulmasova (USSR)   8 33·2

80 metres hurdles sec.

1938	C. Testoni (Italy)	11·6
1946	F. E. Blankers-Koen (Netherlands)	11·8
1950	F. E. Blankers-Koen (Netherlands)	11·1
1954	M. Golubnichaya (USSR)	11·0
1958	G. Bystrova (USSR)	10·9
1962	T. Ciepla (Poland)	10·6
1966	K. Balzer (GDR)	10·7

100 metres hurdles sec.

1969	K. Balzer (GDR)	13·3
1971	K. Balzer (GDR)	12·9
1974	A. Ehrhardt (GDR)	12·66
1978	J. Klier (GDR)	12·62

400 metres hurdles sec.

1978	T. Zelentsova (USSR)	54·89

4 × 100 metres relay sec.

1938	Germany (F. Kohl, K. Krauss, E. Albus, I. Kuhnel)	46·8
1946	Netherlands (G. J. M. Koudijs, N. Timmer, J. Adema, F. E. Blankers-Koen)	47·8
1950	GB (E. Hay, J. C. Desforges, D. G. Hall, J. F. Foulds)	47·4
1954	USSR (V. Krepkina, R. Ulitkina, M. Itkina, I. Turova)	45·8
1958	USSR (V. Krepkina, L. Kepp, N. Polyakova, V. Maslovskaya)	45·3
1962	Poland (M. Piatkowska, B. Sobotta,* E. Szyroka, T. Ciepla)	44·5

* formerly Janiszewska.

4 × 100 metres relay – *contd*   sec.

1966	Poland (E. Bednarek, D. Straszynska, I. Kirszenstein, E. Klobukowska)	44·4
1969	GDR (R. Hofer, R. Stecher, B. Podeswa, P. Vogt)	43·6
1971	Germany (E. Schittenhelm, I. Helten, A. Irrgang, I. Mickler)	43·3
1974	GDR (D. Maletzki, R. Stecher, C. Heinich, B. Eckert)	42·51
1978	USSR (V. Anisimova, L. Maslakova, L. Kondratyeva, L. Storashkova)	42·54

4 × 400 metres relay   min. sec.

1969	GB (R. O. Stirling, P. B. Lowe, J. M. Simpson, L. B. Board)	3 30·8
1971	GDR (R. Kuhne, I. Lohse, H. Seidler, M. Zehrt)	3 29·3
1974	GDR (W. Dietsch, B. Rohde, A. Handt, E. Streidt)	3 25·2
1978	GDR (C. Marquardt, B. Krug, C. Brehmer, M. Koch)	3 21·2

High jump   metres

1938	I. Csak (Hungary)	1·64
1946	A. Colchen (France)	1·60
1950	S. Alexander (GB)	1·63
1954	T. E. Hopkins (GB)	1·67
1958	I. Balas (Romania)	1·77
1962	I. Balas (Romania)	1·83
1966	T. Chenchik (USSR)	1·75
1969	M. Rezkova (Czechoslovakia)	1·83
1971	I. Gusenbauer (Austria)	1·87
1974	R. Witschas (GDR)	1·95
1978	S. Simeoni (Italy)	2·01

Long jump

Year	Athlete	metres
1938	I. Praetz (Germany)	5·85
1946	G. J. M. Koudijs (Netherlands)	5·67
1950	V. Bogdanova (USSR)	5·82
1954	J. C. Desforges (GB)	6·04
1958	L. Jacobi (Germany)	6·14
1962	T. Shchelkanova (USSR)	6·37
1966	I. Kirszenstein (Poland)	6·55
1969	M. Sarna (Poland)	6·49
1971	I. Mickler (Germany)	6·76
1974	I. Bruzsenyak (Hungary)	6·65
1978	V. Bardauskiene (USSR)	6·88

Shot

Year	Athlete	metres
1938	H. Schroder (Germany)	13·29
1946	T. Sevryukova (USSR)	14·16
1950	A. Andreyeva (USSR)	14·32
1954	G. Zybina (USSR)	15·65
1958	M. Werner (Germany)	15·74
1962	T. Press (USSR)	18·55
1966	N. Chizhova (USSR)	17·22
1969	N. Chizhova (USSR)	20·43
1971	N. Chizhova (USSR)	20·16
1974	N. Chizhova (USSR)	20·78
1978	I. Slupianek (GDR)	21·41

Discus

Year	Athlete	metres
1938	G. Mauermayer (Germany)	44·80
1946	N. Dumbadze (USSR)	44·52
1950	N. Dumbadze (USSR)	48·02
1954	N. Ponomaryeva (USSR)	48·02
1958	T. Press (USSR)	52·32
1962	T. Press (USSR)	56·90
1966	C. Spielberg (GDR)	57·76

Discus – *contd*

Year	Athlete	metres
1969	T. Danilova (USSR)	59·28
1971	F. Melnik (USSR)	64·22
1974	F. Melnik (USSR)	69·00
1978	E. Jahl (GDR)	66·98

Javelin

Year	Athlete	metres
1938	L. Gelius (Germany)	45·58
1946	K. Mayuchaya (USSR)	46·24
1950	N. Smirnitskaya (USSR)	47·54
1954	D. Zatopkova (Czechoslovakia)	52·90
1958	D. Zatopkova (Czechoslovakia)	56·02
1962	E. Ozolina (USSR)	54·92
1966	M. Luttge (GDR)	58·74
1969	A. Ranky (Hungary)	59·76
1971	D. Jaworska (Poland)	61·00
1974	R. Fuchs (GDR)	67·22
1978	R. Fuchs (GDR)	69·16

Pentathlon

Year	Athlete	pts
1950	A. Ben Hamo (France)	4023
1954	A. Chudina (USSR)	4526
1958	G. Bystrova (USSR)	4733
1962	G. Bystrova (USSR)	4833
1966	V. Tikhomirova (USSR)	4787
1969	L. Prokop (Austria)	5030
1971	H. Rosendahl (Germany)	5299
1974	N. Tkachenko (USSR)	4776*
1978	M. Papp (Hungary)	4655*

* New Tables.

Heard about the Puffin Club?

...it's a way of finding out more about Puffin
books and authors, of winning prizes (in
competitions), sharing jokes, a secret code, and
perhaps seeing your name in print! When you
join you get a copy of our magazine, *Puffin
Post*, sent to you four times a year, a badge
and a membership book.

For details of subscription and application
form, send a stamped addressed envelope to:

The Puffin Club Dept A
Penguin Books Limited
Bath Road
Harmondsworth
Middlesex UB7 0DA

and if you live in Australia, please write to:

The Australian Puffin Club
Penguin Books Australia Limited
P.O. Box 257
Ringwood
Victoria 3134